D0558423

THE HUMOR
OF JESUS

THE HUMOR OF JESUS

Henri Cormier

ALBA · HOUSE   NEW · YORK

SOCIETY OF ST. PAUL, 2187 VICTORY BLVD., STATEN ISLAND, NEW YORK 10314

Originally published under the title **L'Humour de Jésus** by Editions Paulines, Montreal, Canada.

Library of Congress Cataloging in Publication Data

Cormier, Henri, 1909-
The humor of Jesus.

Tranalation of L'humour de Jésus.
Includes bibliographical references.
1. Jesus Christ--Humor. I. Title.
BT590.H8C6713   232.9'03   77-9887
ISBN 0-8189-0356-2

Designed, printed and bound in the United States of America by the Fathers and Brothers of the Society of St. Paul, 2187 Victory Boulevard, Staten Island, New York, 10314, as part of their communications apostolate.

3 4 5 6 7 8 9 (Current Printing: first digit).

Today, both exegetes and theologians have begun to speak not only of the humor of the sacred writers, but also of the humor of God and that of Christ . . . In the sort of book in which the message of Jesus is made available to the contemporary world in a language which it can easily understand, one religious writer has noted that "humor is never wanting in the Gospel. It arises less frequently from the words themselves than from the context in which they are spoken." How could Jesus have managed to attract children, women, simple people, if he was always aloof and serious? On the other hand, a learned theologian has shown that the instinctive unwillingness most Christians have, in times gone by and today as well, to think of a Jesus who can laugh ultimately derives from the fact that they consider him, in an almost exclusive fashion, as the embodiment of the dogma of the divinity of the Messiah. We have such a vivid awareness of his divinity that we are almost inclined to deny the reality of his human nature.—

Jean Leclercq

PROLOGUE

It is easy to speak of Christian humor, of humor in the Gospel, or in the Bible. But we hesitate to say explicitly that "God has a sense of humor," or "Jesus has a sense of humor." In the three volumes of indices to the periodical **La vie spirituelle,** up to the year 1954, one can notice some articles on the subject of joy, but not a single title which mentions humor. It is also true that there is not a single word about anxiety. Are we to conclude that these are both very recent categories in Christian spirituality? Or is it rather, as frequently happens in an era of renewal, that these are traditional elements which have simply been lost sight of and are being rediscovered little by little?

There was little hesitation at the prospect of discussing the humor of the saints in a pleasant book which appeared on the eve of the Second World War, a book which is relatively little known.[1] With respect to Tauler, one might speak of a gift which is "frequent in the case of the mystic, that of humor, the humor of people who have no illusion about the holiness of their state of life, nor about the ultimate worth of the observances and exercises which they are no less serious in practicing."[2] St. Bernard has left us all the elements of an itinerary which leads "from humor to love."[3] A whole series of

---

1. S. Jacques and R. Keryn de Marcke Ten Driessche, L'humour des saints, Paris, 1939.

2. Cl. Champollion, Six-centième anniversaire de la mort de Tauler, 1361-1961, in Etudes germaniques, 20 (1965), p. 49.

3. Jean Leclercq, De l'humour à l'amour, in Témoins de la spiritualite occidentale, Paris (Cerf), 1965, pp. 264-287.

VIII   THE HUMOR OF JESUS

writings has recently been assembled under the title
**"Humor and Spirituality in the Early School of Saint
Theresa."**[4] It actually would seem as though every authentically spiritual milieu must necessarily produce
humor. A recent book on the subject of humor in the
religious community asks this plaintive question: "Why
is it that a title like **Humor in the Church** has never
been the number-one entry (what an honor that would
be!) in a general collection entitled **Humor;** how many
people would welcome such a book with joy, with
humor!"[5]

Until recently, the subject of humor in the Bible, and
particularly humor in God, in Jesus, was not taken
seriously, if one might put it in these terms. There have
indeed been some pages devoted to the subject of humor
in the writings of Hilaire Belloc, of Romano Guardini,
of Fulton Sheen. But these texts have been considered
simply as amusements, as literary diversions. In 1951,
in the first edition of the **Jerusalem Bible,** the fascicle
on Jonah openly admits, from the very outset, that this
book contains "a certain sense of humor that one is
surprised to discover in the writings of the Bible."[6] In
1961, Daniel-Rops makes mention of "this pleasant sense
of irony which is observable in the manner [of Jesus]."[7]
Speaking of the role which ought to be played by humor
in the process of catechesis, as it is outlined in the Gospels, a recent author adds the comment that "we have
not yet given sufficient attention to the Gospels from
this point of view."[8] In 1968, a book by J. Sullivan notes

---

4. Humor y espiritualidad en la escuela teresiana primitiva, Burgos,
1966.
5. Frère Hilaire, **Humour en Eglise,** Ed. Paulines, 1971, p. 2.
6. **The Book of Jonah,** tr. by A. Feuillet, 2nd ed., Paris, 1957, p. 7.
7. Daniel-Rops, **La vie quotidienne en Palestine au temps de Jésus,**
Paris, 1961, p. 66.
8. A. de Peretti, **Liberté et relations humaines,** Paris, 1966, p. 263.

that "humor is never wanting in the Gospels. It arises
less frequently from the words themselves than from
the context in which they are spoken."[9] In 1970, the
Benedictine Jean Leclercq concludes his book on the
contemplative life with a chapter on the contemporary
role of humor. This is the chapter which has supplied
the introductory quotation for this study, a text which
has also been used by "Christian Readings for our Times."

To my knowledge, there is not a single book which
is entirely devoted to Jesus' humor. There is an English
book by E. Trueblood, **The Humour of Christ,** published
in London in 1965. There is also a book which bears the
title **God Is Funny.** The author explains, "Why this title?
Because it says God without saying God. When we
speak of someone and say that he is funny . . . we are
saying nothing about him; we are only expressing the
fact that there is something funny about him, that he is
'not like everybody else'. . . that he is someone original,
someone whose acts and attitudes are unexpected and
even . . . shocking . . . Understand him if you can. In fact,
it is not even a question of understanding; it is simply a
question of accepting him, making him welcome, being
ready for everything. We have to expect everything on
the part of God; that is the result of his freedom. He is
unpredictable in his words and in his attitude. It remains
for us to laugh, the way a person laughs after a funny
story; not that he has understood it completely, but
rather that he knows what it is about, he sees where it
is aimed; this is the laughter that arises when we have
'caught on.' This is the laughter that brings us up to the
humor of God himself, this God who is so funny precisely because he has loved man to the point of mad-
ness."[10]

9. J. Sullivan, **Dieu au-delà de Dieu,** Paris, 1968, p. 88.
10. François Chalet, **Dieu est drôle,** les Ed. Ouvrières, Paris, 1968,
pp. 5-7.

X   THE HUMOR OF JESUS

Why do we hesitate to speak of the humor of Jesus? A learned theologian has shown that the instinctive unwillingness most Christians have in times gone by and today as well, to think of a Jesus who can laugh, ultimately derives from the fact that they consider him, in an almost exclusive fashion, as the embodiment of the divinity of the Messiah. We have such a vivid awareness of his divinity that we are almost inclined to deny the reality of his human nature.[11] We would be afraid of taking something away from his serious purpose, his dignity, his majesty . . . To say that Jesus laughed, that he had a sense of humor, would be a lack of respect to the Son of God. (It must be noted that even though there is a paragraph on the laughter of Jesus in this book, properly speaking, humor is expressed rather by the smile.)

The ultimate reason behind our repugnance to speak, and especially to write, about the humor of Jesus seems to be our lack of realism with respect to the humanity of Jesus who became "like unto us in all things, excepting for sin." If we think that the saints must have had a sense of humor, if we can write that "it really looks as if every authentically spiritual milieu must produce humor," then why must we refuse this very important quality to Jesus? He is true man and perfect man.

In this present book, we shall make the following points: (1) Jesus had a sense of humor, and one completely devoid of mockery, because he had a sense of the relative, and because he expresses himself in a language that is profound and frequently needs to be understood on several levels of meaning. (2) He enjoys the primacy of humor; he has a perfect humor, because he enjoys primacy in everything, since he is the psycholo-

---

11. F. Jansen, S.J., Jésus a-t-il ri?, in Nouvelle revue théologique, 56 (1929), pp. 367-368.

gist, the pedagogue, the psychiatrist, the sociologist par
excellence, etc. (3) Jesus showed his sense of humor in
dealing with the people. We shall examine various of
the Gospel narratives in an attempt to discover words
or situations which exhibit Jesus' sense of humor. "Seek
and you shall find": if we search for God we will find
him, if we search for love we will find it, and if we
search for a sense of humor we shall find that as well.
We might hesitate in the face of one or another example,
or decide that the author must have exaggerated—and
it is always possible that he has been deceived. But we
do well to trust implicitly in the sincerity of an old professor of Sacred Scripture; we would do well to remember that "humor is never wanting in the Gospels. It
arises less frequently from the words themselves than
from the context in which they are spoken." Neither
should we forget that it takes a sense of humor to find
a sense of humor . . . (4) Jesus shows a sense of humor
with his disciples: think, for example, of the case of
St. Peter. (5) Jesus exhibits his sense of humor to the
very end. It is possible that this prospect will give rise
to "an instinctive repugnance." "A sense of humor at
the Last Supper! On the cross! After the Resurrection!
This certainly goes far beyond what could be expected.
This is too much. Who can stand for this?" Each example
proposed in the following discussion must be judged
on its own merits. But this is the spirit which animates
the entire investigation; it is a theme expressed so well
in Psalm 2 (2-5): "The kings of the earth stand ready,
and the rulers conspire together against the Lord and
his anointed king . . . The Lord who sits enthroned in
heaven laughs them to scorn; then he rebukes them in
anger." Jesus is always "the same," in the most tragic
circumstances and in the most glorious circumstances,
just as he is in the most ordinary situation: full of love
towards us because we have need of him, full of love

also because frequently we do not know that we have need of him, because we do not understand his love, or because we believe that we know, and because we are pretentious, paltry, little, and frequently disobedient. (6) Whatever may be the weaknesses or imprecisions of a book on a subject that is so little studied in Christian literature, I hope that we can agree on one fundamental fact: Jesus has a sense of humor. He wants to show that sense of humor, even today, in us, in our midst: there certainly is a "present-day realization of humor" in our modern age.

This then is the book on the humor of Jesus. By way of presentation, let me paraphrase the prologue of Saint Luke's Gospel (1:1-4): "Since so few people have undertaken to draw up an account of the humor of Jesus, in the events that have happened among us, following the traditions handed down to us by the original eye witnesses and servants of the Word, I have decided, as one who has gone over the whole course of these events in detail, to write a connected narrative for you, so that everyone will know that the Son of God, our Lord and Savior, source of life and light and love . . . is also the source of humor for all mankind and for his saints."

CONTENTS

THE HUMOR
OF JESUS

I.

JESUS HAD A SENSE OF HUMOR

What is a sense of humor? The dictionaries discuss such related terms as humor, jesting, wit, mockery, irony, with the result that, when all is said and done, the reader is no better informed than when he first set out to discover the meaning of humor. The truth of the matter is that humor is a very subtle reality, and very difficult to define. Various formulae have been proposed. We might quote that of J. P. Dubois-Dumée: "The sense of the relative which makes it possible to enjoy a taste for the absolute." It has also been said that humor is not a virtue, but is rather the "radiance of all the virtues," or, once again, that humor exists "when we laugh in spite of everything," especially when we have the skill and grace to laugh at ourselves. Finally, humor has been defined as "an art of living: it keeps everything in its proper place . . . , humor is a quality of love."[1]

We shall attempt rather to discover the nature of humor such as it is exhibited in the character of Jesus. As we watch the God-Man speaking and acting, we shall perhaps arrive at a description of humor in its most perfect expression, humor as lived by the most perfect of men.

We shall discover the following points:

1. Jesus had a sense of humor.

---

1. J. Op de Beeck, "Pour une plus large ouverture dans la communauté religieuse." in Carrefour des religieuses, Malines, p. 29.

2. Jesus frequently makes use of irony.

3. Jesus does not use mockery.

4. Probably Jesus laughed.

5. "Double meaning" is a key to Jesus' humor.

6. The secret of Jesus' humor is his sense of the absolute and of the relative.

1. Jesus had a sense of humor

Jesus had a sense of humor and still has one. To choose to make himself man, when he is God! To be willing to spend his life as a carpenter, a drinker of wine, even a blasphemer—does this not call for a sense of humor?

There is humor in the fact that he came to dwell among men, knowing full well that he would never be received. He came to tell us that he loves us, and that we should love each other just as he loves us. This is a serious message and one that cannot be understood by those who take themselves too seriously. That is why Jesus set about communicating his message of love to us with a considerable amount of humor.

There is humor in the comparisons employed by Jesus: "You strain out the gnat, yet swallow a camel! . . . You see the speck in your neighbor's eye, but you do not see the two-by-four in your own . . . A man does not put new wine into old wineskins . . ." (Mt 23, 24).

There is a sense of humor, and frequently an incisive one, in the stories (parables) which he tells: "If your hand or your foot is your undoing, cut it off and fling it away . . . If it is your eye that is your undoing, tear it out and fling it away" (Mt 18:8). All this is exaggerated. But everybody understands. And the man who does not take himself too seriously will recognize that the hat fits.

Jesus injects a sense of humor into his relationship

with the apostles, so vain, so pretentious: "What were you discussing along the road?" He catches them red-handed like naughty children caught in the very act of misbehaving: "They kept silent, for they had been discussing along the road which of them was the greater" (Mk 9:33).

Jesus also showed his sense of humor in his dealings with women. With the Samaritan woman: "Go get your husband," even though he knows full well that she has five husbands (Jn 4:16). To the woman with the hemorrhage who comes up behind to touch him: "Who touched me?" although the crowd was pressing against him on every side (Lk 8:44). With Martha, who is concerned with many preparations for a grand "lunch": "Martha, Martha, only one or two things are needed" (Lk 10:41).

There is also a sorrowful sense of humor in Jesus. In the Garden of Gethsemane, suffering from a terrible anxiety and actually sweating blood, he goes to seek a little sympathy from his three favorite apostles and finds them asleep. "From now on you can sleep and take your rest. Behold, the hour has come when the Son of Man is going to be delivered to the hands of sinners" (Mt 26:45). Irony? Let us rather call it sadness, understanding, and forgiveness.

On the cross (yes, even there), there is a sense of humor born of mercy and forgiveness. To the criminal who asked Jesus to remember him in his kingdom, Jesus answers "Indeed, I say to you, this very day you shall be with me in Paradise" (Lk 23:43). Here is a man who stole on earth and now has managed to steal heaven—with the connivance of Jesus himself!

After his resurrection, Jesus shows a sense of humor in the way he reveals himself. As the first messenger of his Resurrection, he chooses Mary Magdalene, from whom he had cast out seven devils (Jn 20:17). Thomas refuses to believe before putting his finger into the wounds of Jesus' hands. "Although the doors were locked, Jesus came and stood among them, saying, 'Peace be with you.' Then he said to Thomas, 'Reach your finger here; see my hands. Reach your hand here and put it into my side. Be unbelieving no longer, but believing'." It does not say that Thomas actually put his finger into the wounds. But, in his complete bewilderment, he pronounces the most beautiful profession of faith in all the Gospel: "My Lord and my God!" (Jn 20:24-28).

In this present book, I should like to convince myself further, and to convince the reader as well, that Jesus loves us. I should like to help us, you and me, to cast off our own self-sufficiency, to say with Peter, after all our denials, "Lord, you know everything, you know that I love you" (Jn 21:17).

Jesus treats us with humor, because he surpasses us, because he understands us, because he takes our measure and loves us. We, on the other hand, have very little sense of humor, because we are very little and yet we think we are very grand. A man who has a sense of humor can perfectly well understand a man who has none. The man who has none can never really understand the man who has a sense of humor, but he pretends to understand everything, because he does not understand enough. Jesus understands men: "He knows what is in the heart of man" (Jn 1:25). But men, for their part, "see without seeing and hear without understanding" (Mt 13:13).

Jesus had a sense of humor, and he still has it.

2. Jesus sometimes makes use of irony

Jesus' humor is filled with love and hope. What we call **black** humor is born of despair: this is the humor that sees man as egotistical and vain, which regards the human condition as mired down in evil and suffering, destined to existential nothingness; what it necessarily experiences is "nausea." Black humor teaches us that "other people—that is hell," that "it is not worth the effort to live," that "only suicide makes any real sense." This is the logic imposed by an "absurd" nature and a cruel destiny. Both of these kinds of humor have a certain logic. But one is optimistic while the other is pessimistic; one has the long-range view, while the other is short-sighted.

Jesus is the most rational of men, because he is the Man-God. He realizes that man is egotistical, but he teaches man to try to be something else. A gloomy sense of humor would encourage man to be as egotistical as possible, to see love, for example, as nothing more than sexuality, simply a matter of hormonal chemistry.

Jesus realizes that man must die. But he wants to bring man the hope of resurrection. His humor springs from a complete understanding of man and his destiny. Black humor claims to be perfectly rational and clear, but it is lacking in perspective, and thus its vision is faulty. Its proponents "have become futile in their thinking and their senseless minds have been darkened. Claiming to be wise, they have become fools" (Rm 1:21). The humor of these "philosophers and wise men" is something incomplete and akin to despair. The humor of Jesus is complete, filled with hope, because he knows the whole of man.

English humor is frequently distant, haughty, cold. The humor of Jesus is always affectionate, smiling, warm. It comes from a loving heart. For Jesus, humor is a trait associated with love. It is an appeal to the heart of "the victim," even though the victim itself might not understand until "later," as happened so frequently in the case of Peter (Jn 13:6). Jesus' humor comes from the heart and appeals to the heart.

Sometimes Jesus makes use of irony. His irony

springs from his love, but from a love which has encountered an obdurate refusal, a categorical opposition, a mortal hate. Jesus' irony is reserved for his implacable opponents: the Pharisees and the Scribes, the Sadducees and the Herodians, who were the intellectuals and theologians, the priests and the politicians, in a word,' the "experts," of his day. Jesus' irony is meant to pique, . . . but also to convert: this is the ultimate instrument of his love, to arouse a human freedom that has closed itself against him.

There is probably irony when, on the evening of the Last Supper, Jesus tells Judas: "What you are going to do, do quickly" (Jn 13:27). And again, at the moment of his arrest, in Gethsemane: "Judas, would you betray the Son of Man with a kiss?" (Lk 22:48).

Jesus' humor is addressed to those who are not yet fixed in their evil, to those who have good will, to the simple, to the "babes" (Lk 10:21), even if they are still living in sin, like the publicans and prostitutes. Speaking of these to the Pharisees, Jesus says: "They will enter before you into the Kingdom of Heaven" (Mt 21:31).

Jesus' irony is reserved for those who have bad will, for the obdurate, for the "wise men" who rationalize and justify their position: "If you were blind, you would have no guilt; but now that you say, 'We see,' your guilt remains" (Jn 9:41).

Love knows how to tease a friend, how to point a finger at his defects, at his pettiness, his vanity, at the paltriness of a man who "would like" to love our Lord, the man who would like to "understand" the mystery of Jesus. Irony makes a mockery of pride, hypocrisy, the hate that shuts up within itself and claims to be sufficient unto itself. Irony can go so far as to include a curse: "Woe to you, scribes and Pharisees, hypocrites . . . blind guides . . . whitened sepulchres . . . " (Mt 23: 13-27).

When addressed to a "mixed" audience, made up, on the one hand, of the little people and publicans, and, on the other hand, of the great teachers of the Law and the Pharisees, the same gestures, the same words of Jesus can sometimes contain humor for the one group and irony for the other. Thus, for example, with respect to the tribute owing to Caesar: "Render to Caesar what is Caesar's, and to God what is God's." The Pharisees are dumbfounded. "They could find no fault with his words before the people, and, taken by surprise, they held their peace." But everyone else welcomed his answers: "The great throng heard him gladly" (Mk 12:37).

3. Jesus does not make use of mockery

In Jesus, both humor and irony come from love. In Jesus, there is no trace of mockery, for mockery is born of hate and triumphant pride. Jesus' opponents are the mockers: "So also the chief priests, with the scribes and elders, mocked him, saying, 'He saved others; he cannot save himself. If he is the King of Israel, let him come down from the cross, and we will believe in him. He trusts in God; let God deliver him now, if he wants him; for he said, I am the Son of God' " (Mt 27, 41-43).

Jesus' humor and irony are something light. Black humor and despondent irony are lucid up to a certain point. Mockery, on the other hand, proceeds from hatred, and hatred makes it blind. This is a term which occurs frequently in Jesus' speech to characterize his enemies: "They are blind men leading blind men" (Mt 15:14). "Woe to you, blind guides . . . foolish and blind" (Mt 23: 16-24).

Humor is luminous: "I am the light" (Jn 8:12). Mockery is darkness: "The light has come into the world, and men loved darkness rather than light, because their deeds were evil. For every one who does evil hates the light, and does not come to the light, lest his deeds should be exposed" (Jn 3:19-20).

Humor is both benevolent and beneficent; mockery is malevolent, cruel, and malicious. Humor is smiling; mockery grinds its teeth (Ac 7:54). Humor is cordial and serene; mockery is bitter and bilious. Humor sows joy; mockery sows sadness.

4. Did Jesus laugh?

There was once, in a Church setting, an attempt to conduct a "serious" debate, "without humor," and according to the rules, on the subject: "Did Jesus laugh?" The negative was proposed by a "pessimist," while the affirmative was argued by an "optimist."

The pessimist argued as follows: (1) Jesus was too serious and too austere to laugh. (2) Laughter presupposes a certain abandon, a sense of surprise, a lack of control, and none of this could possibly exist in the perfect man that is Jesus. (3) Throughout his entire life, Jesus was preoccupied with the suffering of his Passion, which dominated his horizon. (4) It is written in the Book of Sirach that "a fool raises his voice when he laughs, but a clever man smiles quietly" (21:20). (5) Jesus says of himself: "My soul is very sorrowful, even to death" (Mk 14:34).

In support of the affirmative position, the "optimist" responded as follows:

1. Serious does not mean sad and austere. Serious is opposed to frivolous, silly. Jesus was always serious, for he had a perfectly clear awareness of all of reality around him, and his reaction to every circumstance was always perfectly appropriate.

2. Even though, by virtue of the fact that he was God, Jesus knew everything, still, in so far as he was also a man, his intelligence, his imagination, his emo-

tional potential all developed in terms of new experiences: "Jesus increased in wisdom and in stature, and in favor with God and man" (Lk 2:52). Even if Jesus knew everything and could not be surprised by anything, there were still situations in which he could indulge in wonder. Thus, faced with the centurion's faith, "He marveled, and said to those who followed him, 'Truly, I say to you, not even in Israel have I found such faith' " (Mt 8:10). Admiration is not necessarily the same as surprise. Properly speaking, it is a sense of marvel in the face of a great and beautiful reality, of the type that is not frequently encountered.

3. If Jesus was thinking of his passion, he also proclaimed his resurrection (Mt 16:21; 17; 22; 20; 19).

4. The Book of Sirach does not say that the "wise man" does not ever laugh, but rather that his laughter is controlled, seldom, and discreet.

5. If Jesus was sad under certain painful circumstances, such as in the Garden of Gethsemane (Mk 14:34), still his life was filled with joy which resulted from his union with his Father. He goes so far as to say that he has come in order to share his joy with us: "So that my joy may be in you, and so that your joy may be complete" (Jn 15:12). Joy is the awareness of the presence of a pleasant reality and the feeling of fullness which follows upon this awareness. The joy of Jesus was always complete, at least in the upper levels of his awareness: "I am not alone; the Father is with me" (Jn 16:32).

The negative arguments having been thus swept aside, reduced to ashes, and cast to the winds, the affirmative position advanced two "serious" arguments which completely knocked down the opposition and reduced the pessimist position to a shambles.

In the Sermon on the Mount, often referred to as the Magna Carta of Blessedness, Jesus speaks against those who "look dismal," or "disfigure their faces." He recommends that they "anoint their heads and wash their faces" (Mt 6:16-17).

Jesus took part in the marriage festival at Cana. Now, everybody is in a good mood at a wedding feast. It would appear, at least at the wedding feast of Cána, that Jesus did laugh.

It is probable that he also laughed on other occasions: for example, when James and John wanted to have fire come down from heaven on a village in Samaria which refused to let the band of Apostles pass through (Lk 9:54), the occasion on which he gave them a new nickname, "sons of thunder" (Mk 3:17); when the comrades of the paralytic took the tiles off the roof of the house where Jesus was staying and let their friend down through the hole (Mk 2:4); when Martha was upset at the fact that her sister Mary was doing nothing to help her. While she was working all alone in the kitchen, her sister was sitting down and simply listening to what Jesus said (Lk 10:41).

We might indeed suppose that Jesus frequently spoke "with a smile," in a pleasant tone, with a serene and jovial expression, with a spark of humor in his clear, deep eyes. It would be instructive, from this point of view, to re-read the first chapter of St. John (35-51). Let us attempt to reconstruct Jesus' attitude, expression, tone of voice, when he speaks to John and James who are asking him, "Where do you live?": "Come and see" (39). When he says to Simon: "You are Simon, the son of John: You will be called Cephas" (42). When he speaks of Nathanael in his absence: "While you were under the fig tree, I saw you" (48). Reading these passages with careful attention, we ourselves might well be inclined to smile. Actually, it is the entire Gospel which we must read in this light.

Lord, I know that you have a sense of Humor.

You used to smile, in fact you used to laugh out loud . . . Give me the gift of humor, teach me to smile and to laugh.

This is a gift which comes from your own presence, a gift which gives consolation, encouragement, dynamic force . . .

Give me all this, for myself and for the other people as well.

5. A key to Jesus' sense of humor: "the double meaning"

Jesus says to Peter: "You are a hindrance to me; your thoughts are not those of God, but those of men" (Mt 16:23). Naturally our thoughts are those of men. To have the thoughts of God, we must have some form of revelation. In Jesus there are two forms of thought: the thought of men and the thought of God. In him, the thought of God raises up, transforms, and makes divine the thought of men. Jesus speaks to us in the words of men, but it is God who is speaking to us of things divine, profound, mysterious. What we need in order to understand them is not a lexicon or a dictionary. Above and beyond the words themselves, there is the person speaking, who is the Word, who knows all things, who loves, who wants to reveal to us the realities that we could never discover for ourselves.

Jesus speaks with the simplest of words, with the most common-place comparisons, accessible to everyone; but at the same time they express the most profound truths, the most divine meaning. The limited human words he uses are thus possessed of an infinite meaning. He makes use of the words of earth as if they were rockets, to transport us bodily into the "height and depth and breadth and width of love" (Ep 3:18).

He endows these words with many meanings: first
of all the obvious, literal, natural meaning: this is the
level of meaning at which his addressee frequently stops,
making no attempt to go on, asking nothing further,
refusing to knock at the door. This is the reaction of
the man who has no sense of humor, who is satisfied
with the superficial, the partial and incomplete, the man
who has no taste for something better.

There is also, and primarily, the deeper meaning, the
"supernatural meaning," the "meaning" which is beyond
all meaning, the reality towards which Jesus means to
lead the listener who has good will, the man, who, by
the grace of the Father and the Spirit (Mt 16:17), has an
intuitive grasp of the uncharted depths, the man who
questions, and receives the Master's clear and open explanation: "When his disciples asked him what this parable meant, he said, 'To you it has been given to know
the secrets of the kingdom of God; but for others they
are in parables, so that seeing they may not see, and
hearing they may not understand'" (Lk 8:9-10). Let us
note that Jesus speaks of "knowing" these mysteries,
and not of "understanding." "To know" in the language
of Jesus, does not mean to have an intellectual possession, but rather to have a communication, to be open to
a reality which surpasses human understanding. We
might plunge deep into the ocean, frolic and gambol in
its waves, enjoy the awareness of its immensity: but it
is impossible to swallow the ocean.

The following are some of the key words in Jesus'
language. The fact that there is more than one level of
meaning, the presence of something to be understood,
something read between the lines,—this often becomes
a source of humor. The reason is that our Lord's thinking goes far beyond the thinking of men.

"Destroy this sanctuary: in three days I will raise it
up again" (Jn 2:19). The Jews think of the Temple at

Jerusalem: "It took 46 years to build this sanctuary and are you going to raise it up again in three days?" (20). But he was thinking of the sanctuary of his body, greater than the Temple, in fact, the very first temple of God, the place for adoration in spirit and in truth (Jn 4:23). His disciples were to understand all this, but much later, three years later, when Jesus rose from the dead (Jn 2:22).

"Unless he is born again from on high, no one can see the kingdom of God" (Jn 3:4). Nicodemus, even if he is a doctor of theology, takes this word literally, finding it strange, in fact, absurd: "How can a man be born again once he has grown old? Is it possible he can enter for a second time into his mother's womb and thus be born?" Jesus smiles, for he is speaking of Baptism, the new birth in virtue of which the believer approaches the dignity of adoptive son of God: "Unless he is born again of water and the Spirit, no one can enter the kingdom of God."

"He would have given you living water" (Jn 4:10). The Samaritan woman thinks of the water which is in the well, and answers: "Sir, you have nothing to draw with, and the well is deep; where do you get that living water?" (4:11). The Savior is speaking of grace, the vital divine dynamism which will be spread throughout the hearts of the faithful: "The water that I shall give him will become in him a spring of water welling up to eternal life" (4:14).

"The bread of God is that which comes down from heaven, and gives life to the world" (Jn 6:33). His listeners presume that he is speaking of bread which is baked in the oven: "Lord, give us some of this bread" (6:34). But Jesus is speaking of himself: "I am the bread of life." He is speaking of his own person: "The bread which I am going to give is my flesh for the life of the world . . . He who eats me will live through me . . . He who eats this bread will live forever" (vv. 51, 57, 58).

"Our friend Lazarus has fallen asleep, but I go to awaken him out of sleep" (Jn 11:11). His disciples answer him: "Lord, if he has fallen asleep, he will recover." Jesus meant to speak of the sleep of death, but they supposed that he was speaking of a normal night's sleep.

"And I, when I am lifted up from the earth, will draw all men to myself" (Jn 12:32). He was speaking of his being raised up on the cross: he meant, by these words, to explain the kind of death he was to die (12:33). He was also speaking, even more so, of his "being raised up" into heaven, his glorification, his Ascension: "I am going to my God and your God."

"He began to wash the disciples' feet" (Jn 13:5). Peter sees this as a rite of purification, preparatory to sharing Jesus' friendship and eating the Passover with him: "Lord, not my feet only but also my hands and my head!" Jesus explains that what is involved is an example that is to be imitated: "If I then, your Lord and Teacher, have washed your feet, you also ought to wash one another's feet. For I have given you an example, that you also should do as I have done to you" (vv. 14, 15).

Jesus has something very profound to tell us. He knows all the secrets of God, and all our most intimate aspirations, those that are hidden even from ourselves. When he speaks, he makes us search into the very depths of our soul: "Ask, and it will be given you; seek, and you will find; knock, and it will be opened to you . . . . If you then, who are evil, know how to give good gifts to your children, how much more will the heavenly Father give the Holy Spirit to those who ask him!" (Lk 11:9-13).

To have a sense of humor means to be spiritual, to have the spirit; in Jesus, the fullness of the Spirit exists, bodily. True, total humor necessarily implies the presence of the spirit, and the Spirit as well.

Lord Jesus, you are a marvelous presence of the

spirit and of the Spirit.
You speak to us of divine realities in the words
    of men.
Give us the good things of the Father.
Give us the spirit and the Spirit.

6. The secret of Jesus' humor: his sense of the absolute and the relative

In order to have a sense of humor, there has to be a sense of the absolute and the relative. Jesus lived among people who were searching, and among people who pretended that they were already in possession. He promised those who were searching that they would find, those who were asking that they would receive. But Jesus also encountered men who preferred the darkness of the relative to the clear light of the absolute, men who found their absolute in a simple pleasure, in an idea, in one of their fellow-men, whom they could transform into an idol. On such occasions Jesus' humor comes to the fore, and sometimes his irony.

The absolute is the total, lasting, and unchanging reality. The relative comprises all other partial, temporal, and changing realities, whose being, goodness, truth, and duration are all "relative" to the absolute.

Jesus knows what is absolutely good, absolutely true, absolutely lasting. And thus he treats with humor or with irony all those who treat as absolute that which is, in reality, only relative. To those who have too simple a definition of the good, he says "No one is good but God alone" (Lk 18:19). To those who are too inclined to separate the good from the evil, he recommends: "Let the weeds and the good grain grow together until the harvest time" (Mt 13:30). To those who believe that fortune is a lasting gift, he gives this advice: "Fool, this very night your soul is required of you" (Lk 12:20). To those who think they know everything: "You are a teacher in Israel, and you do not know these things!" (Jn 3:10). To those who want to understand everything all at once: "You shall understand later" (Jn 13:7).

The absolute is Somebody. It is not something, not even a perfectly clear idea or a universal principle. The absolute is God, and the Son of God who became man. Here below everything changes, excepting for Jesus who is "the same yesterday, today, and forever" (Heb 13:8). Here below, everything is relative to that one absolute which has made his home among men.

The truth is Jesus. The way is Jesus. The life is Jesus: "I am the way, the truth, and the life" (Jn 14:6). He goes so far as to call himself existence itself: "Before Abraham was, I am" (Jn 8:58). Jesus said "I am." We, on the other hand, can barely say "we have." Jesus is absolute: we are relative to him.

Whoever has a sense of the absolute can clearly see what is relative, and thus possess a true sense of humor. But the man who does not recognize or refuses to know the absolute can only pretend at spirit, can only practice mockery: he has no true humor.

The absolute is the treasure, the pearl for which a man will sell everything that he owns (Mt 13:44-46).

Lord Jesus, you are the only absolute, with your
    Father and your Spirit.
Teach us to search for this one thing necessary,
    with joy and with serious intent.
Teach us to make use of the relative, with humor.

II.

JESUS IS NUMBER ONE IN HUMOR

Perhaps we have encountered people who have spirit or who like to pretend that they do. We may have encountered examples of black humor, English humor, mockery, teasing, or irony. But no one has so complete and open and warm and loving a sense of humor as Jesus. And if any person has any small portion, this all comes from Jesus, who is its ultimate source.

The following are some reasons for assigning Jesus the primacy in humor:

7. Because he is the number-one psychologist;
8. Because he is the number-one pedagogue;
9. Because he is the number-one psychiatrist;
10. Because he is the number-one sociologist;
11. Because he is the number-one journalist;
12. Because he is the number-one worker;
13. Because he is the number-one boss;
14. Because he is the number-one caricaturist;
15. Because he is the number-one in everything.

7. Jesus is the number-one psychologist

He knows what is in the heart of man (Jn 2:25).

Jesus is the number-one psychologist because he knows perfectly what is going on inside man, and he has no need for anyone to instruct him. In order to have a sense of humor, a person has to be a good psychologist.

A perfect sense of humor presupposes a profound awareness, not only of one's self and others, but of God as well.

The psychologist knows and analyzes the inner workings of the human soul. He knows the dynamism of the forces that are at work within a human being and their consequences in the make-up of his personality. He studies the mechanisms of thought and emotional reaction, conscious or unconscious, the moods and motivations behind every form of action and behavior. Psychology is a human science, and thus it is capable of being constantly perfected. Specialists do not always agree, and it is only normal for there to be several schools of psychology, all of them different, and frequently contradictory.

Jesus was a superb psychologist. As a matter of fact, he is the number-one psychologist, because he is number-one in everything (Col 1:18; cf. no. 15). He has a school, and that school is never deceived: "Lord, to whom shall we go? You have the words of eternal life" (Jn 6:68). The reason for his superior sense of psychology is that he is the very one who has made man "in his own image." Thus he understands all the nuances, the most intimate depths of the ego, the conscious and sub-conscious, even the "super-conscious" of faith, hope, and charity, all the defense mechanisms and identification mechanisms, all the sincerity and hypocrisy.

King David stood in admiration before the range and scope of the divine knowledge, and he celebrates God's perfect grasp of psychology, which is also the psychology of Jesus: "Oh Lord, thou hast searched me and known me . . . Thou discernest my thoughts from afar . . . Thou art acquainted with all my ways. Even before a word is on my tongue, lo, Oh Lord, thou knowest it altogether . . . Such knowledge is too wonderful for me; it is high, I cannot attain it . . . For thou didst form my inward parts, thou didst knit me together in my mother's womb" (Ps 139). And by way of conclusion: "I praise thee, for thou art fearful and wonderful. Wonderful are thy works" (v. 14).

Today psychology is very popular. It is increasing our understanding of man, and thus it can accomplish great good. We like to know what is inside us, and inside other people. The courses in our schools that treat the subject of personality attract great numbers of people. It is possible to leave the studies more dynamic, more efficient, and more charitable. But, alas, it is also possible to leave these courses simply more snobbish, more vain, thinking that we understand "everything that is in the heart of man," or woman, or the authorities. We must never confuse knowledge and life, psychology and spirituality. To know oneself and to know other people is a gift which must serve one single purpose: to love oneself properly, to love other people well, to love the way Jesus has loved us, and loves us still.

Two of the Evangelists have perhaps understood our Savior's fine sense of psychology better than the others. St. Luke, a doctor (Col 4:14), had completed a long series of studies on some relatively profound aspects of psychology. St. John, in his Gospel, reveals many profound aspects of Jesus that no one else has called attention to. His remarkable knowledge of the Savior has been attributed to the special influence of Mary, Mother of Jesus, with whom he lived for many years as her adoptive son (Jn 19:26). Many people think that it was from her he got his profound awareness of the hidden depths in Jesus' words and actions, a profundity which has earned his Gospel the title of "Gospel of the Heart of Jesus." We might also call his Gospel the "Gospel of the Heart of Mary."

From the very beginning of his Gospel, John tells us something that he himself had progressively discovered: "He knew all men and needed no one to bear witness of

man; for he himself knew what was in man" (2:25).
Peter is to say in his turn: "Lord, you know everything,
you know that I love you" (Jn 21:17). Jesus knew men;
he is the number-one psychologist: That is why he treats
men with humor.

> Lord, you know everything:
>> You know that I am trying to love you.
> I am blessed indeed,
>> that you know me from the bottom up.
> Make me know you,
>> in order to love you more.
> Make me know other people,
>> to love them like you.
> Make me know myself,
>> to love myself better . . .
> with a bit of humor.

8. Jesus, the number-one pedagogue

Come, follow me (Mt 19:21).

Jesus is the number-one pedagogue, because he
knows from experience the path which leads man to his
total destiny. He goes on in front, inviting us to follow
him, and he does so with humor, because, as we sing
in the popular song: "We all would like to go to heaven,
but no one wants to die . . ."

There are pedagogues who speak the truth but do not
practice what they preach (Mt 23:3). Our Lord tells us
that we are to listen to them, but not to imitate them.
"The scribes and the Pharisees sit on Moses' seat; so
practice and observe whatever they tell you, but not
what they do; for they preach, but do not practice"
(Mt 23:2-3).

Jesus himself is an example of doing what he says:

"I have given you an example, that you also should do
as I have done to you" (Jn 13:15). He himself suffered
before preaching the Gospel of the Cross. He himself
died before teaching us how to die: "A servant is not
greater than his master. If they persecuted me, they
will persecute you" (Jn 15:20).

There are pedagogues who do not know where to
lead people, pedagogues who have no "mystique." They
ask questions, but they have no answers. Or rather,
their answers are incomplete, unlike the answer that
God has revealed to man.

Jesus came so that man could "have life, abundantly"
(Jn 10:10). Jesus guides those who follow him to the
fullness of love: "In order that the love with which thou
hast loved them may be in them, and I in them" (Jn
17:26). The company of Jesus is the true happiness:
"Father, I desire that they also, whom thou hast given
me, may be with me where I am, to behold my glory
which thou hast given me in thy love for me before the
foundation of the world" (Jn 17:24). Every form of
pedagogy which does not envision this fullness of faith,
hope, and charity, is a limited pedagogy, incomplete,
short-sighted; taken for an absolute, it can only produce
tragic results. It amounts to being involved with "blind
guides . . . who shut the kingdom of heaven against men;
they neither enter themselves, nor allow those who
would enter to go in" (Mt 23:13-16). Our Lord also says:
"Can a blind man guide another blind man? Will they
not rather both fall into the pit?" (Lk 6:39).

Jesus tells us clearly where he means to lead us. To
arrive at our goal it is enough to follow him. But Jesus
is a realist; he knows that the road is long and difficult,
and that is why he tells us: "If any man would come
after me, let him deny himself, and take up his cross
and follow me" (Mt 16:24). We say: "We do not know
where Jesus wants to lead us" (Jn 14:5); as a matter of

fact, we know only too well, and we do not want to understand.

It is here that we catch sight of Jesus' humor—a humor that is, for us, something of a paradox. The utopian pedagogues have proposed the prospect of a life on earth without suffering, filled with pleasure, egotistical and without any self-denial. But the reality has not changed for all that: We cannot avoid all suffering, any more than we can avoid death.

Man wants happiness, right away; but Jesus says "later" (Jn 13:36). Man seeks to flee from suffering; Jesus invites us to bear suffering in company with him. Man pursues pleasure; Jesus shows us the cross. It is in this way that Jesus is a realist. He promises us, beginning already on earth, here and now, a hundredfold reward (Mk 10:30), a joy, a peace, but "not as the world gives" (Jn 14:27). He goes so far as to claim that we will always have poor people in our midst (Mt 26:11), that there will always be crosses to bear, suffering and death. Each one of us, with the realism and humor of this Christ who teaches us to see everything as relative, must learn to bear his own cross—realizing that Jesus is carrying the cross together with him, towards his final destiny, just as, along the road to Calvary, Jesus and Simon carried the same cross (Mt 27:32).

Jesus did not come to earth in order to do away with suffering and death, but rather to teach us how to bear suffering and how to live death. He promised that he would be there with us: "I am with you always, to the close of the age" (Mt 28:20). His presence, realized in faith, is the joy and peace which he gives us here below: it is worth a hundred times more than the pleasure and comfort which the "world" has to offer.

This is the realistic and complete pedagogy which Jesus proposes to us with love and humor. He presents it in what seemed to us to be paradoxes, for we are slow to understand (Lk 24:25), because "our thoughts are not those of God, but those of man" (Mt 16:23).

> Lord, you are my shepherd;
> I shall not lack for anything.
> Lord, you lead me
> along the green pastures.
> You guide me along the path of righteousness,
> for your name's sake.
> Even though I walk through the valley of the
> shadow, I fear no evil. (Ps 23)

9. Jesus, the number-one psychiatrist

Your sins are forgiven (Lk 5:20).

In a situation which is not without its humor, Jesus demonstrates that he is the most perfect healer of the guilt complex, and thus the number-one psychiatrist.

The scene is at Capernaum, in a house which might well have been that of St. Peter. There is a crowd within, at the door, and at the windows as well. Some people suddenly arrive carrying a paralyzed man on a stretcher. They try to make their entry in order to place the unfortunate man at Jesus' feet. Since the door and windows are blocked by the crowds, the stretcher-bearers climb onto the roof, remove some of the tiles, and, through the hole they have thus made, let down the litter by ropes into the room below, where they trust the poor man will be helped. We can imagine the amazement and amusement of all present, and also the indignation of the owner at this strange invasion of his privacy. Jesus sees all this as a splendid act of faith. He smiles (or laughs) at the originality of their approach.

Everyone is expecting that the paralytic will be cured. Jesus, however, does not seem to be concerned with the man's illness. He sees a much deeper evil, the man's sinful condition: "My friend, your sins are forgiven." By his sin, man separates himself from God, and yet Jesus addresses him as "My friend." The scribes and Pharisees, like good theologians, immediately begin to reflect: "Who can forgive sins, but God alone?" The principle behind their reasoning is true, but their logic is false. They refuse to recognize, in fact they deny, that Jesus is God, and thus able to forgive sins. Jesus reads their thoughts. He tells them: "Which is easier to say: Your sins are forgiven? Or: Get up and walk?" A man can say both these things easily enough, but only God can both say and produce either the pardon or the cure, just as he brings all creation into being by his word. "Very well, in order that you might know that the Son of Man has power on earth to forgive sins, I command you—and this he says to the paralyzed man—get up, take up your stretcher, and go back home." And at that very instant, the paralytic stood up before their very eyes, picked up the stretcher he had been lying on, and went back home glorifying God.

Let us note that Jesus never told anyone to lie down on the analyst's couch. A young lady who was once invited by her psychiatrist to lie down on the couch, cried out in objection: "Oh no! That is where all my problems came from." When Jesus finds a person lying on his bed or stretcher, he usually tells him to get up, especially if it is a woman, as in the case of Peter's mother-in-law (Mk 1:31). If she is a young person, he takes her by the hand to help her to her feet (Lk 8:55). If it is a man, Jesus tells him to pick up his bed and go his way, as in the case of the paralytic just described.

In the amusing situation just recounted, Jesus clearly showed himself to be God, having the power to forgive sins here upon earth. St. Matthew (9:8) reports the reaction of those who witnessed this event: "When the crowds saw it, they were afraid, and they glorified God, who had given such authority to men." As a matter of fact, the man Jesus does have such a power, and he wants to share it with other men. On the evening of his resurrection, he is to appear to his apostles, breathe upon them and tell them: "Receive the Holy Spirit. If you forgive the sins of any, they are forgiven"—this is the sacrament of forgiveness (Jn 20:22). It is a reality from a higher order, but not one that contradicts our human reason. It forces us to give glory to God for having given such authority, such power to men.

Every Christian is a sinner who has been forgiven. Jesus does not take away the sense of guilt, but he does absolve the sinner. It is no true service to try to take away the sense of guilt, when the fault is real and actual. It is a lack of realism. What the guilty person needs is conversion and forgiveness, with the clear recognition of his responsibility. Every other remedy is artificial, a deceptive bandage over the reality of a sinner who has not been converted, and a bandage that is not destined to last. Sin is not a sickness; it is an evil for which we are responsible.

Our Lord has known all about depth psychology for a long time, in fact, from all eternity. He came down upon earth in order to give us the most effective form of psychotherapy, together with the divine power of forgiveness. There is nothing so valuable in this connection as the words: "My friend, your sins are forgiven you."

Lord, you are the number-one healer:
    You forgive me.
    You ask me to forgive.
I thank you.
Grant me the gift to forgive myself.

10. Jesus, the number-one sociologist

I shall build my Church (Mt 16:18).

Jesus is the number-one sociologist because he has founded an eternal society, one which will unite all men from every nation. Complete humor presupposes faith in, hope for, and love of, the total society in which man lives and will continue to live.

A university professor began his first lecture in sociology as follows: "In order to be a sociologist, a person needs three qualities: faith, hope, and love. Faith in himself, in others, and in God. Hope in himself, in others, and in God. Love of self, of others, and of God." This is what Jesus has come to tell mankind, to teach them his sociology.

Jesus has come to live among us in order to found a society, a kingdom, a community, a church: "You are Peter, and upon this rock I shall build my church, and the powers of the Evil One will not prevail against it" (Mt 16:18). This is a strange society. It does not fit into a category of our modern sociology. It surpasses all of them. It is not a monarchy, and yet it has a King. It is not a democracy, and still it is the People of God. Whenever we try to label it, we do it an injustice. We must not confuse our human sociology with the Kingdom of God.

Jesus entrusts his society to men. What faith in mankind! What hope! What love! What a sense of humor! And still, the very first pope is destined to deny him. The very first bishops are destined to abandon him. Over the course of centuries, how many denials, how many defections, how many deviations, on the part of Christians, big and small alike. Still Jesus dares to claim: "The powers of the Evil One shall not prevail against it."

The society of Jesus (and here we are not speaking of the society founded by St. Ignatius) is at one and the

same time visible and invisible. It is interior, within
each individual man: "The kingdom of God is within
you" (Lk 17:21). It has an external organization, with
its leaders, its pastors: "He who hears you, hears me"
(Lk 10:16). It has a position within time: it is a field in
which weeds and good grain are growing together (Mt
13:30); it is a net which gathers all sorts of things, good
and evil alike (Mt 13:47). It will also have a prolongation
into eternity, which will be inaugurated by the burning
of the weeds and the harvest of the good grain (Mt
13:30), by assigning one group to eternal suffering and
the other to eternal life (Mt 25:46).

It is a just society in which it is really true that the
poor will be rich, and that the unhappy will be happy
(Mt 5:3ff.). It is a universal society which embraces all
men, all nations of all the earth, of all time.

The sociology taught by Jesus surpasses all human
sociologies, in time and in duration, in space and in
immensity. It is more than cosmic (no. 15). Though incarnate, it is also transcendental; it is in the world, but
it surpasses the world (Jn 18:36). Jesus is the first king
who does not have an earthly army, commanding instead all the legions of heaven (Mt 26:53). He is the
first to announce, for himself and for his followers, that
suffering must come before reward, and death before
resurrection. He is the first to claim that authority is not
lording it over someone, but rather being a servant (Lk
22:24-27). He is the first head of a society to proclaim the
imperfection of his work in time and his subjects' lack
of understanding (Jn 13:6). Jesus' society is the only
society which will make men perfectly happy, without
a utopia and without any deceitful promise: "He who
follows me will not walk in darkness, but will have the
light of life" (Jn 8:12). Jesus says what he sees (Jn 1:18).
And what he says "enlightens every society and every
man" (Jn 1:9).

Jesus is the number-one sociologist because he has faith in his Father, in himself, and in man; because he hopes in his Father, in himself, and in man; because he loves his Father, himself, and man.

He is sure of his society: "I shall build my Church, and the powers of the Evil One shall not prevail against it." He is sure of his word: "Heaven and earth shall pass away, my words shall not pass away" (Mk 13:31).

> Lord, I believe in your Church
>   on earth and in heaven.
> You have entrusted it to men,
>   limited and sinners,
>   weak and vain . . .
> What a great risk you have taken,
>   with a bit of humor . . .
> May your kingdom come
>   on earth as in heaven!

11. Jesus, the number-one journalist

Proclaim the good news! (Mk 16:15).

Jesus is the number-one journalist because he announced the good news. A complete sense of humor always implies something good to say. Jesus announced the good news par excellence, and he asks us to proclaim it to every nation. This reality, always good and always new, is the fact that God loves us; that God is with us; that God wants us to be with him, happy forever.

When my duties required that I deal with young people, I used to repeat to them frequently "God loves you. I love you too." But first they used to answer me "We know that you love us. But why not leave God out of it?" And then one day "We are beginning to understand that by loving us, you are making us realize that God loves us too." And finally, one day a young man caused me great joy by completing my thoughts for me: "Why don't you add: Love each other?" And thus the refrain became the following: "God loves you; I love you; let us love each other." This is what Jesus came to tell us. This is the good news. This is the Gospel, and it deserves to be printed in our newspapers, in big block letters, banner headlines.

There are some journalists who think they "have" the truth. Jesus, however, "is" the Truth (Jn 14:6). There are journalists who refuse to name their sources, true or imaginary. Jesus is an honest and authentic journalist: he always gives his source: "My teaching is not mine, but his who sent me" (Jn 7:16). He reports exactly what he has heard and seen: "I have not spoken on my own authority; the Father who sent me has himself given me a commandment what to say, what to speak" (Jn 12: 50). If you have listened to a press conference or have been a witness to some event, and if, on the following day, you read the newspaper report, how often do you not find that the event had been "filtered" or "biased" by the very headline itself, and in the narrative that follows?

Someone has said: "The real news is not the news that you find in the papers." Good news is rare. What we find is mostly bad news: "Everything is going poorly." "Men are wicked." "God is dead." "Everyone for himself." "Winner take all."

No one has ever spoken as Jesus has (Jn 7:47). The crowds were astonished at his teaching, for he taught them as one who had authority, and not as their scribes" (Mt 7:28). The scribes used to repeat the doctrine of the great teachers in Israel: they were afraid to change anything, to add anything, to invent anything. Jesus, on the other hand, renews everything. He does not abolish the

Law and the Prophets, but he fulfills them, and leads them to the point of love (Mt 5:17). He is a real journalist who helps his hearers to advance towards an understanding of the truth by reporting the whole reality, just as it really is. His sermons are editorials which are valid for all time, and for all men. His great by-line is always: "God loves you. I love you. Love each other." As a matter of fact, this good news is not something, it is Some One: it is Jesus himself. It is himself that he has come to proclaim, for the good of all mankind. "Proclaim the Good News."

> Lord, I find it hard to believe
>   in the Good News:
> I read so much bad news.
> Help me to believe in love.
> Help me to spread the Good News,
>   with a little bit of your humor.

12. Jesus, the number-one worker

I also work (Jn 5:17).

Jesus is the number-one worker, because "all things were made through him, and without him was not anything made that was made" (Jn 1:3). The man who works has the right to exercise his sense of humor, and if his humor is involved and responsible, there is a chance that it will be true. The lazy man is a source of irritation right and left, just like a stubborn fly; he criticizes, gets people angry, and claims for himself the glory of other people's success, even though he has done nothing but spur them on.

Jesus, although he was the son of God, still worked with his hands. He was known as "the carpenter, the son of Mary" (Mk 6:3). He lived for thirty years at Nazareth,

where he was at first simply an humble apprentice, a
helper, before he took over Joseph's shop, upon the
death of his adoptive father. He knows what it means
to "bear the burden of the day's work, with its heat"
(Mt 20:12). He is not unfamiliar with the injustices
practiced by many subordinate bosses who "begin to
beat the menservants and the maidservants, and to eat
and to drink and to get drunk" (Lk 12:45). Jesus sets
himself up as the defender of the working man: "Come
to me, all you who labor and are heavy-laden, and I will
give you rest. Take my yoke upon you, and learn from
me; for I am gentle and lowly in heart, and you will
find rest for your souls. For my yoke is easy, and my
burden is light" (Mt 11:28f.).

With his own hands, Jesus accomplishes great marvels (Mk 6:2). He takes a young twelve-year-old by the
hand and restores her to life (Mk 5:41). He puts his fing-
ers into the hands of the deaf-mute, touches his tongue
with his saliva, and the man begins to speak correctly
(Mk 7:33f.). He touches and heals both blind and leper.
He lays his hands upon the sick (Mk 6:5). But it is primarily upon the cross that Jesus really worked "manu-
ally," when they drove the nails through his hands.

"My father is working still, and I am working" (Jn
5:17). Jesus' work, like that of his Father, is a total and
complete work. Men on earth accomplish only partial
work, whether it be with their hands, their minds, or
their creativity. Jesus is working on the whole of man,
the whole of nature, the whole cosmos, the whole of
everything. He heals men's bodies in order to save the
whole man forever: "Just as the Father raises the dead
and gives them life, so also the Son gives life to whom
he will" (Jn 5:21). For him, this means working in his
Father's vineyard, gathering the scattered flocks, build-
ing up the Kingdom of Heaven.

This is something of what we must understand when

he says: "I must work the works of him who sent me" (Jn 9:4). "I too am working."

> Lord, you are the number-one worker.
>   You love the worker.
> Help me to love
>   work and workers.
> Give me the gift of working together with you,
>   with your love and with your sense of humor.

13. Jesus, the number-one boss

Go, you too, into my vineyard (Mt 20:4).

Today, it takes a great deal of humor to say anything good of our boss. It is fashionable to say that the boss has every possible defect and vice, that he commits all manner of injustice; that no matter what, he is wrong. But I should like to claim that there is at least "one" good boss: Jesus and his Father; that there is one boss who has a sense of humor: Jesus. Jesus used to tell the crowds many stories: they were called parables. In the parable of the workers in the vineyard (Mt 20:1-6), the owner goes out early in the morning to hire laborers for his vineyard. In those days, the place where the laborers would gather to be hired was the village square: anyone who wanted to work would assemble there. On this particular day, the "morning shift" was hired for a twelve-hour day, from six to six. They signed on (elective bargaining?) for a denarius, something like 35 cents: in the salary scale of those days, this was a good price, before inflation. The laborers are satisfied.

Around 9:00, the owner makes a second appearance in the marketplace and sees some other men who do not yet have any work, standing there idle; probably they "slept in" that morning. He tells them: "You, too, go into my vineyard, and I will give you whatever is a just salary." It must be noted that there is no collective bargaining in this time: the laborers trust themselves to the boss's sense of justice. Fortunately, the leaders of our labor unions seem never to have heard this parable. Finally, the owner goes out again towards noon, and again at about 3:00, to do the same thing.

Around 5:00, he makes one final trip and finds still other workers: They must have been taking most of the day off, but had still come to the marketplace, after 3:00, in the hope of earning a few pennies. These, too, are invited to work in the vineyard, without any bargain having been struck.

When evening comes, at 6:00, the owner tells his overseer to give each man his wages: workers were paid at the end of each day; there was no job security, and no deductions on their wages. The reckoning begins with the latecomers, those who were hired at 5:00, and they receive a denarius, the wages for a whole day's work. When those from the morning hiring come, they think they are going to receive more, but they receive, as agreed upon, just one denarius, like everyone else. It was too late to go on strike, but at least they could complain, protest, raise the issue: "Injustice! Down with the boss! Unfair working practices, unfair wages!" They threaten to take the whole business to the grievance board. One great big strong fellow takes the lead and complains louder than all the others. The owner addresses his remarks to this man: "Friend, I am doing you no wrong; did you not agree with me for a denarius? Take what belongs to you, and go; I choose to give to this last as I give to you. Am I not allowed to do what I choose with what belongs to me? Or do you begrudge my generosity?" The story does not go on to say whether there was a commission to investigate, or a "spontaneously" organized demonstration, to take action against this boss, this "establishment" figure who had thus abused the lot of the poor defenseless proletariat.

What Jesus is teaching here is that God is a good boss. His primary intention is to tell the Jews, who have been serving God from the early morning of history, that they will indeed have their recompense, but that they must not be jealous when others enter into the Kingdom, barbarians and pagans, our ancestors and we ourselves, the "civilized" peoples of the West. There are people who have been working for him from the early morning of their life, baptized in their infancy. By their agreement, by the New Testament, they will have heaven as their recompense. There are people who do not encounter the Lord before the eleventh hour of their life. But God, in his goodness, will also give them the recompense of heaven. This is how the good thief, on Calvary, actually stole Paradise (no. 55).

A person has to be very good, and the person has to have a little, in fact perhaps a lot, of humor, in order to reveal all this to people who are so petty, and so jealous.

Lord, you are my boss and my brother.
Give workers and bosses
    the gift of uniting in your justice and your
    goodness.
Give me the gift of working for social justice
    with your love and with your humor.

14. Jesus, the number-one caricaturist

They disfigured their faces (Mt 6:16).

The Gospels never mention that Jesus wrote anything, excepting perhaps in the account of the woman taken in adultery: "Jesus bent down and wrote with his finger on the ground" (Jn 8:6; no. 21). Even here, the

Gospel writer does not satisfy our curiosity: he does not tell us what was written.

If Jesus does not write, he still manages to describe vividly in words, with a truly divine art. He is the perfect portrait painter; he seizes upon the true and fundamental characteristics of people, and describes them in sober, brief, and frequently incisive terms, to the great enjoyment of the crowds. He describes the sower (Mt 13:13), the woman who was baking bread (Mt 13:13), the woman who was sweeping out her house (Lk 15:8), the merchant (Mt 13, 45), the lilies of the field and the birds of the air (Lk 12:27). In a word, Jesus can conjure up an entire picture, a complete situation: "No man ever spoke like this man" (Jn 7:46).

Jesus excels in his caricature of the hypocrites, that is, the scribes and Pharisees. If caricature is a reproduction of a person or a thing, by sketch, description, or drawing, with some satirical or humorous intention, then Jesus, through his words which surpass every form of pictorial art, is the number-one caricaturist.

As for his "victims," he describes them with marvelous accuracy—the external: "When you fast, do not look dismal, like the hypocrites, for they disfigure their faces that their fasting may be seen by men" (Mt 6:16);— vanity: "When you pray, you must not be like the hypocrites; for they love to stand and pray in the synagogues and at the street corner, that they may be seen by men" (Mt 6:5); "they do all this in order to be seen by men."

Such people are hypocrites, in the face of men and in the face of God. Their pretentious conduct and their self-satisfaction know no limits. In this connection, we must think of the story of the Pharisee and the publican (Lk 18:9-14). The passage needs to be read aloud (like all the other words of our Lord, for that matter), slowly, with proper pauses, in order to savor all the details, for every word means something: "Two men went up into the temple to pray, one a Pharisee and the other a tax collector."

Let us examine the Pharisee: "The Pharisee, with his head held high, prayed thus within himself, 'God, I thank thee that I am not like other men, extortioners, unjust, adulterers, or even like this tax collector . . . I fast twice a week, I give tithes of all that I get . . .' "

Let us examine,the publican: "But the tax collector, standing far off, would not even lift up his eyes to heaven, but beat his breast, saying, 'God, be merciful to me a sinner'." Lafontaine could not have said it any better.

Finally, a few days before his death (probably on Tuesday of Holy Week, April 4, in the year 30 A.D.)[1] Jesus apostrophizes and caricaturizes the scribes and Pharisees, in a passage which has been called the "seven woes" (Mt 23:13-32): "Woe to you, scribes and Pharisees, hypocrites. You close the Kingdom of heaven to men. You do not enter yourselves, and you do not let those go in who want to. You devour the widows' houses, and for a pretence make long prayers (Mk 12:40). You are like whitewashed tombs, which outwardly appear beautiful, but within they are full of dead men's bones and all uncleanness. Blind guides. Vipers, brood of vipers. How are you to escape being sentenced to hell?" It is a frightening proclamation. "Then he will speak to them in his wrath, and terrify them in his fury" (Ps 2:5).

Indeed, Jesus is the number-one artist, portrait painter, caricaturist.

Lord, you are the Word par excellence.
Help us to speak a little bit like you,
    to help our brethren live,
    with love and humor.

---

1. The dates suggested here are only probable. They are given in order to help the reader to "realize" that Jesus really lived on this earth at a definite time and place.

15. Jesus, number-one in everything

That primacy may be his in everything (Col 1:18).

One might continue this list of Jesus' first places, and say, for example, that he is the number-one doctor, a title which he can claim for several reasons (Mt 9:12; Lk 4:23; 5, 31). With a little bit of humor, we might even add that he is the number-one botanist (Lk 12:27), the number-one ornithologist (Lk 12:24), even the number-one veterinary doctor (Lk 14:5), etc.

But all these distinctions which we have described up to this point are really only "partial" first places. They all have to go together in order to have a complete, a perfect sense of humor, which can locate every person, every event, every finite being properly in its relationship with the infinite. In Jesus, all these claims to first place arise from the fact that he possesses the fullness of all things, in its first source and in its highest form.

St. Paul says of Jesus: "He is the head of the body, . . . the beginning, . . . that in everything he might be pre-eminent" (Col 1:18). In the Book of Revelation (22:13), St. John puts these words into Jesus' mouth: "I am the alpha and the omega, the first and the last, the beginning and the end."

1. Jesus is the first-born of all creation (Col 1:15). The Gospel of St. John says: "In the beginning was the Word, and the Word was with God, and the Word was God" (1:1).

2. Everything was created in him, through him, and for him (Col 1:15f.). "In" him, for it is in his image that everything has been made: it is in him that the Father, the divine architect, first formed the plan and idea of everything in heaven and on earth (v. 20); "through" him, for everything was made through him, and without him nothing was made (Jn 1:3); "for" him, everything

bows down at the name of Jesus, in the very heights of heaven, upon earth, and in the world below (Ep 2:10).

3. Everything subsists in him (Col 1:17). This means that every being, every form of life, every thought in every act of love, every activity at all exists only because of the fact that Jesus, the Man-God, constantly supplies everything with being, life, thought, love, activity. "He is the first principle" (v. 18).

4. He is the head of the body (v. 18): That is, he is the head of the kingdom, of the people of God, of the community, the society, the Church, which he animates and makes ready in this world of time, with all its imperfect men, and which he will one day lead to perfection in the world after this time, or better, eternity, where he will present to his Father his people, mankind, like a bride "in splendor, without spot or wrinkle or any such thing, that she might be holy and without blemish" (Ep 5:27).

5. He is the first-born from among the dead (Col 1:18). He is the first to be raised, opening the grand procession of all the dead who will come back to life through the dynamic power of his resurrection (Rm 8:11).

6. All the fullness of God was pleased to dwell in him (Col 1:19). All the fullness of everything lives in Jesus, and from his fullness we all receive (Jn 1:16). This means first of all the fullness of divinity, for the full divinity of God dwells in him (Col 2:9; Jn 10:10). What is more, we must also think of the fullness of cosmic reality: the universe, the whole cosmos is filled with his power and his presence as creator, preserver, and giver of dynamic life. For Paul, the Incarnation, crowned by the Resurrection, has placed Christ's human nature at the head of not only the whole human race, but also the whole created cosmos. We are speaking of "the cosmic Christ," whose breadth and length and height and depth and love surpass all understanding (Ep 3:18-20).

St. Paul does not cease to marvel at this immensity, this fullness of the Man-God. This vision of his opens up upon an infinite horizon. It was destined to be contemplated and explained by a number of Christian thinkers, among others by Teilhard de Chardin. According to St. Paul, we can enter into all the fullness of God through Christ who lives within our hearts, by being firmly rooted in love, by the power of the Spirit (Ep 3:17-19). We can even act with the very dynamism of Christ the Man-God: "To him who by the power at work within us is able to do far more abundantly than all that we ask or think, to him the glory . . ." (v. 20).

Lord, you are number-one in everything.
You are the source
    of every being and every dynamism,
    in us, in every one,
    on earth and throughout the cosmos.
To you be glory,
    today and forever.
Make us dynamic,
    for you and for everyone,
    with your love and with your humor.

III.

JESUS' HUMOR WITH PEOPLE

Jesus loved people and crowds. He was happy to be surrounded by "the simple and lowly," to teach them whenever he had an opportunity. Still, he was always careful to be very clear, recognizing the limitations of his audience, their whims and their lack of understanding. This concern was frequently manifest in a smiling and benevolent form of humor towards them (nos. 16, 31).

16. Humor[1] plays a pious trick

The wedding at Cana (Jn 2:1-12).

Mary had just told Jesus: "They have no more wine." Jesus answers her in his Aramaic language: **"Mali walaq,"** which the Jerusalem Bible translates as "What do you want of me, woman?" The question corresponds more or less to our familiar expressions: "Well what then? So what?" It is an oral expression that has many meanings: only the context, the facial expression, the tone, the circumstances can determine the concrete meaning which can range, according to the individual case, all the way from anger, insult, contemptuous refusal, all the way to humor, all the way to a gracious and familiar

---

1. "Humor, written with a capital letter, is to be understood as referring to the personification of humor in the person of Jesus. God is Love. Jesus refers to himself as the Life, the Way, the Truth, the Shepherd, the Vine, the Resurrection, etc. I would go so far as to add that Jesus is Humor."

invitation, such as one would expect between people who love each other.

At the wedding feast at Cana, we might be inclined to translate: "What can we do about it, madam?"—giving the word "woman" a playful and somewhat affected meaning. The answer could thus take on the appearance of a refusal. But Mary understands it so well that she interprets it, correctly, as consent. The prayer surest to be heard is that which submits in advance to anything that Jesus wants. That is why Mary tells the servants, "Everything he tells you, do it."

Jesus' sense of humor here combines with the humor of his mother Mary, in the affectionate trick which they play together on the newly married couple, on the wedding guests, and the master of ceremonies. Jesus changes the ablution water into wine (almost a hundred gallons of it). "When the steward of the feast tasted the water now become wine, and did not know where it came from (although the servants who had drawn the water knew), —they were in on the trick, and were enjoying the humor of the situation—the steward of the feast called the bridegroom and said to him, 'Every man serves the good wine first; and when men have drunk freely, then the poor wine. (This is a trick that we are not unfamiliar with from our modern bars and restaurants). But you have kept the good wine until now'." When Jesus makes something, it is bound to be good.

Mali Walaq: "What can we do about it, Madam?" These words express an attitude which governs the love and humor of Jesus and Mary throughout their life, not only at Cana and during the years of his public life, but also throughout the long centuries of mankind's pilgrimage on earth, until the time of the eternal marriage feast, when the best wine will finally be served. It is an action on the part of Jesus which is discreetly encouraged by his mother Mary.

There are also a few servants who know the true origins of the water and wine of their good turns, done out of love and humor.

Lord, you can change water into wine.
    You can also change wine into your blood.
Mary is always with you,
    discreet, benevolent, maternal.
Jesus and Mary, change us,
    make us willing to serve people,
    with a little bit of your humor.

17. Humor is not naive

Jesus did not trust himself to them (Jn 2:24).

Jesus is in Jerusalem for the Passover (probably March or April of the year 28). After seeing the marvels which he accomplished, many people believed in his name. But Jesus "did not trust himself to them, because he knew all men and needed no one to bear witness of man" (no. 7).

Why did Jesus refuse to entrust himself to those who were declaring for him? The answer is that their faith and their conversion were neither true nor authentic. They admired Jesus for speaking and acting with authority, for performing wonders. They were drawn by his strong and charming personality. Deep down inside, they were asking themselves if perhaps this were not the Messiah announced in prophecy and eagerly awaited. "Let us be on his side. Let us follow him. Let us become his disciples." But what they are really looking for is their own self-interest: they want to make use of him, not to be his servants. Everyone is thinking of his own future. Perhaps they can manage to achieve a good position in his kingdom . . . This is the way in which

James, John, and their mother will understand the Lord (Mt 20:20; no. 45). It is advantageous and intelligent, in fact it smacks of the avant-garde, to follow a future victor, a conqueror, and perhaps even a future king. But when they are placed before the "mystery of Jesus," when they have to opt for a true faith which demands a gift of all their life and the renunciation of their own self, these same people will say: "These words are too strong. Who can bear them?" (Jn 6:60; no. 38).

There have been, in the history of Christianity, conversions and vocations that were dictated by economics, politics, social status. When the Church was a power, when the nations were Christian, it could be of great advantage to believe in Christ, even to be a devotee of Christ, . . . but of which Christ? We have perhaps all known some business people who used to go to Mass because it was profitable for their business. We might well ask whether the Christianity of certain politicians was not really a matter of politics. There have been many salesmen who took advantage of an uncle who was a priest, an aunt who was a nun, to sell their products to churches and to religious communities. We might even suppose that certain vocations to the priesthood or the sisterhood were more or less deliberate attempts to seek out a privileged situation or a secure old age. Recent history can only make us think.

We do not have the right to judge these matters: Jesus remains the only judge. But what the Gospel tells us is that in certain cases "Jesus did not trust himself to them." There are still some "Christians" who are trying to make use of him rather than to serve him. They are not authentic, they are not really "turned" towards him, Christocentric; they are egocentric, self-centered: they are turned towards themselves. A person with a sense of humor does not let himself be caught, does not let himself be used. Humor is not naive.

Oh Jesus, you know the heart of man.
Give me the gift of being mistrustful of myself.
Forgive me my egotism and my self-centeredness.
Draw me to yourself,
    so that I may truly turn towards you.
Help me to become authentic,
    with a little bit of humor.

18. Humor asks, in order to give

Give me to drink (Jn 4:1-15).

Jesus' conversation with the Samaritan woman is a remarkably beautiful little vignette. One hardly knows which to admire more: Jesus' fine sense of psychology, the open and sincere attitude of the woman, the give and take of their conversation, the depth of his ultimate revelation.

The scene is set at Sichar, a village in Samaria, not far from Jacob's well. It is about noon. Jesus, tired from his traveling, has sat down near the well. He is alone: his disciples have gone into the village to buy provisions. A woman of Samaria approaches, with a water-jar on her head. She has come to draw water. Jesus begins the conversation: "Give me a drink." This is a natural enough request, in the heat of the midday sun. In the East, no one refuses water, even to his worst enemy. But this simple request is destined to launch a lengthy conversation.

The woman is surprised, but she is used to talking to men. She is not at all embarrassed. Her language is relaxed, fluent, and subtle. As a Samaritan, she has some pointed remarks to make about the Jews. A true dialogue soon develops between Jesus and her. Our Lord always stays close to people and to the things of earth, even while he is elevating the conversation to the most sublime revelations. Her answer is somewhat haughty and even mocking: "What? How is it that you, a Jew, ask a drink of me, a woman of Samaria!" Jews and Samaritans had no dealings with each other. The Jews considered Samaritans as schismatics, "as born of fornication" (Jn 8:41), and avoided even speaking with them, so as not to be "contaminated." The woman thus savors the mischievous pleasure of sarcasm, and at the same time makes the most of her flirtatious opportunity to offer her service as a favor.

Jesus answers tit for tat: You think that you are giving me a gift, but actually it is I who am giving a gift to you. He begins by exciting the woman's curiosity: "If you knew the gift of God, and who it is that is saying to you, 'Give me a drink,' you would have asked him and he would have given you living water'." The woman has understood Jesus' point, and is curious about his identity, but she is unwilling to betray this curiosity, even though she is burning with it. What he means to say by "living water" she cannot possibly understand, nor is she particularly interested in understanding; but she does not mean for him to have the last word. Her answer is a mixture of irony, independence, and a certain respect: "Sir, you have nothing to draw with, and the well is deep; where do you get that living water?" She is right: even today, the water in this well is about 90 feet below the surface. She has a rope to draw the water with, but Jesus has none.

Still this man intrigues her: he is not just anybody. His subtle mind and his calm and noble expression suggest an insidious question which will lead him to reveal his true identity: "Are you greater than our father Jacob, who gave us the well, and drank from it himself?" Whom do you claim to be?

Jesus holds off for the moment the revelation of his true identity. For the time being, he pursues the revelation of the "living water": "Everyone who drinks of this water will thirst again, but whoever drinks of the water that I shall give him will never thirst; the water that I shall give him will become in him a spring of water welling up to eternal life." Today we can recognize the fact that Jesus was thinking of and preparing the revelation of that profound and dynamic and divine life which is bestowed far and wide by the Spirit in the hearts of those who believe.

The Samaritan woman, for her part, knows nothing of all this; she cannot get beyond the surface of things; she is bound to the literal meaning of Jesus' words. But she shows herself to be very practical, somewhat amused, in fact, a little bit sarcastic: "Sir, give me this water, that I may not thirst, nor come here to draw."

What a freedom that would be, to no longer have to face a long and arduous task in going to draw water. Ultimately, the woman must suspect that what is involved is something deeper, that she does not understand. But if this gentleman wants to continue the conversation, he is going to have to express himself more clearly.

> Lord, you frequently start a conversation
> > with a request for something to drink or
> > something to eat.
> Give us the gift of responding well to your requests.
> Give us the gift of having a thirst for you,
> > for your love, for your humor.

19. Humor reveals the truth in the heart

You are right in saying, "I have no husband"
(Jn 4:16-42).

The Samaritan woman is trying to avoid the heights

to which Jesus' conversation is trying to lead her, and at the same time she desires to enjoy the exchange further. Jesus, for his part, wants to lead her back to herself through the realization of his true identity: "Go, call your husband, and come here." This is an order whose eventual consequences were perfectly well-known to Jesus. The woman's reply is brusque and quick: "I have no husband." It is a bit of easy deception on her part.

Jesus takes her up on it: "You are right in saying, 'I have no husband'; for you have had five husbands, and he whom you now have is not your husband; this you said truly." The Lord stresses what was true in her answer; he avoids telling her that she is wrong, that she has lied; this would have put her off. In saying that she does not have a husband, she has said the truth, for the man with whom she is living now, after five previous husbands, is not really her husband.

The woman is deeply touched by this. She becomes serious. Seeing that she is perfectly known and understood, she recognizes the presence of a man of God: "Sir, I see that you are a prophet." Implicitly she admits her equivocal situation. It is a sort of "confession." Her understanding of Jesus' identity is progressing: he is and remains "Sir." But now she also recognizes him as "prophet." Soon she will take yet a further step.

But she remains a woman. Instinctively, she tries to change the direction of a conversation which is working to her disadvantage and embarrassment. Let us speak of something else; let us speak of religious controversies. The Samaritan woman points a finger to Mount Gerizim, clearly visible from Jacob's well: "Our fathers worshipped on this mountain; and you say that in Jerusalem is the place where men ought to worship." The underlying meaning is this: And you, what have you got to say? Jesus affirms the Jewish claim to precedence:

"Salvation is from the Jews." But he also adds that this does not oblige a person to become a Jew, nor even to worship at Jerusalem: "Woman, believe me, the hour is coming when neither on this mountain nor in Jerusalem will you worship the Father. The hour is coming, and now is, when the true worshippers will worship the Father in spirit and truth."

This is some consolation for the woman: there is no longer any obstacle to her faith: she can believe and still remain a Samaritan, she can worship where she wants, in spirit and in truth. A Jew who exhibits such a broad view of things might well be the Messiah. She speaks of his coming, but at the same time it is a question: "I know that the Messiah is coming (he who is called Christ); when he comes, he will show us all things." Jesus confirms her suspicion: "I who speak to you am he." Blessed is she who has understood, she who has believed in the word which was spoken to her.

We would like to see this conversation carried further. But the disciples arrive and put an end to it: twelve Jewish men, bearded, Galileans, quarrelsome and disputatious by reputation: this was obviously too much Jewish representation for the woman: "She went away into the city." Nor should we forget this detail: "Leaving her waterjar." Was it because of her hurry? Was it a feminine ruse? When she returns, she will be able to use this as a pretext: "I forgot my waterjar."

The Samaritan woman turns into a missionary: "Come, see a man who told me all that I ever did. (She has no shame!) Can this be the Christ?" The people from the village come out to the well; perhaps one or another of her five or six husbands is among them. They beg Jesus and his followers (a band of Jews!) to stay with them.

A good number of people from the village believed in him "because of his words to her." And they said to the woman: "It is no longer because of your words that we believe, for we have heard for ourselves, and we know that this is indeed the Savior of the world." There is no reply on the part of the Samaritan woman. Her role is finished: she is willing to disappear, and there is no further mention of her in the Gospel narratives. She leaves all the glory to the Lord, the Prophet, the Messiah, the Savior of the world. Wonderful Samaritan woman! Wonderful Jesus!

> Jesus, you are my Lord and my Savior.
> Turn me into your missionary:
>> To tell my brethren who you are.
> Make me disappear,
>> So that you can appear.

20. Humor dispells darkness from our hearts

Let him who is without sin among you be the first to throw a stone at her (Jn 8:2-11).

This event takes place during the Jewish feast of Tabernacles (probably October 18-20, 29 A.D.). Jesus had passed the preceding night on the Mount of Olives. At dawn, he went to the temple, and all the people gathered around him. He sat down and began to teach. He was interrupted by the arrival of the scribes and the Pharisees, elbowing their way through the crowd with a great fuss and disturbance, well aware of the fact that they were accomplishing the work of Yahweh, and intent on showing off their purity and piety to all. They are pushing a woman before them, and they cast her down at Jesus' feet. Then, standing on their dignity, they tell the Savior: "This woman has been caught in the act of adultery." There is no mention of her accomplice: presumably he has made his escape.

"Now in the law Moses commanded us to stone such.

What do you say about it?" They have prepared a clever trap. It is a dilemma: Jesus must either join with them in condemning the unfortunate woman, and join them in stoning her, thereby contradicting in his actions what he has been teaching in his words—or else, in front of all these people, Jesus must openly proclaim his contempt for the morality expressed in the law of Moses, and thus his prestige is at an end. "What do you say? You who eat with sinners and with prostitutes!"

Jesus does not answer. He stoops down and begins writing with his finger on the ground. (What did he write? We could advance a lengthy list of conjectures that have been offered, and then end up with the learned conclusion that "We simply don't know." I should prefer to begin where others end: "I don't know.")

Meantime, the scribes and Pharisees are insistent in their demands. Then Jesus turns to them and says: "Let him who is without sin among you be the first to throw a stone at her." Then he stoops down once again and starts writing on the ground again. With a few well-chosen words, Jesus has forced each person to recognize, deep within his own conscience, the presence of him in whose name they meant to perpetrate this atrocious deed, him whose presence they have conveniently forgotten: God. God to whom each one of these people has so frequently proved unfaithful, and who—for who can say?—had perhaps himself accomplished, in secret, the very act for which he now publicly reproaches this woman. Does it not often happen, in our modern society, that certain young people condemned to "re-education," certain "prostitutes" who have been put into prison, have actually been judged by the very people who have contributed to their moral undoing?

The prospect of condemning someone else for the evil we commit ourselves tends to ease one's conscience. But Jesus throws a clear, harsh light on the entire business. The shadows which blinded the eyes of this woman's accusers are now scattered, and, with them, their self-justification has disappeared. They discover that they have sinned themselves. For the first time, perhaps, they perceive God as he really is: as him who gives man his law, but also as one who forgives.

These simple words of Jesus are like a judgment: they bring out the full truth. And still, they do not express either a sentence or a condemnation: "When they heard it, they went away, one by one, beginning with the eldest," who were perhaps the most guilty, or perhaps simply the wisest. They withdrew both themselves and their condemnation, or perhaps one might say that they took the condemnation upon themselves.

Jesus remained alone with the woman, who was still there, crouching on the ground before his feet. Jesus looked up and saw her: "Woman, where are they? Has no one condemned you?" "No one, Lord." "Neither do I condemn you; go, and do not sin again." Humor does not condemn; it invites conversion.

Lord, you do not condemn.
　You forgive,
　You invite conversion . . .
Give me the gift of not ever condemning,
　Of not ever casting the stone,
　Not the first stone,
　And not any other stone.

21. Humor thinks about the mother

Jesus gave him back to his mother (Lk 7:11-17).

We are now in Naim, a little village to the south of Tabor, in the plain of Esdralon (and the time is July, A.D. 28). This, or so it seems, is the first of the three resurrections worked by Jesus (cf. nos. 22 and 23).

Jesus had just approached this little city called Naim. His disciples and a great throng of people were traveling together with him. Now when he got close to the city gate, they were conducting a funeral, outside the city, the only son of a mother who was a widow. And there was a considerable crowd of people with her.

Upon seeing her, our Lord had pity on her and said: "Do not weep." Then he came up, touched the bier, and the bearers stood still. He said: "Young man, I say to you, get up." The dead man sat up on the bier and began to speak.

Then "Jesus gave him back to his mother." This is a touching detail, characteristic of the Savior's kindness. Humor thinks of the mother.

Lord, you had pity on this mother,
    perhaps because you have a mother too.
Give to mothers of all living children . . .
Give to all mothers everywhere
    A little of the love and humor
    that your mother has.

22. Humor does not forget those who are hungry

He ordered them to give her something to eat
(Lk 8:40-56).

This event takes place at Capernaum (around December of A.D. 28). A man by the name of Jairus, chief of the synagogue, casts himself at Jesus' feet and begs him to come to his home, because his only daughter, twelve years old, is dying. As he sets out, the crowds pressed about him. It was on this journey that the woman with the flow of blood came up and touched him (no. 27). While they were on their way, a messenger came to tell

Jairus: "Your daughter is dead; do not trouble the Teacher any more." But Jesus, who had heard this, answered him: "Do not fear; only believe, and she will be well."

Arriving at the house, he allows no one to enter with him, excepting Peter, James, and John, the same disciples whom he chose on Tabor (no. 41), and at Gethsemane (no. 50), as well as the child's mother and father. Everybody was weeping and lamenting for the girl. "Do not weep; for she is not dead but sleeping." Before raising Lazarus from the dead, Jesus expresses himself in much the same manner: "Our friend Lazarus is sleeping: I am going to wake him up" (no. 23). For Jesus, death is only a sleep from which a person can awaken through the power of God. The mourners laughed at him, knowing full well that the child is dead. He has them all put outside (Mk 5:40).

He goes into where the child is lying, takes her by the hand, and says: "Child, get up." Her spirit returns and at the very instant, she gets up. The apostles and her parents are seized with wonder. They can hardly believe what they see. After some hesitation, they touch her, ask her to speak, to get up and walk.

Jesus observes the scene. Everybody is excited about the child. He is the only one who keeps his presence of mind, and what he says is put so simply and in such a practical way: "He directed that something should be given her to eat." Enough now: she is hungry, poor child. This is down to earth: this is divine humor, and divine teaching at work. How often do we want to enjoy a child's presence or conversation, but he is hungry, or he wants to play. The little girl was well served, we may count on that. Watching her eat with hearty appetite, one could certainly tell that, beyond a doubt, she was very much alive. After his resurrection, Jesus was to demand in his turn: "Do you have anything here to eat?" (Lk

24:41). When we eat, we can be sure that the body is alive.

Jesus does not ever forget to feed those who are hungry (no. 37). The day will come on which he gives himself as food (no. 39).

> Lord, you think of everything.
> Whether we are eating,
>> Whether we are drinking,
>> No matter what it is that we are doing,
> We want to do it all in your name,
>> And for the glory of your Father,
>> With love and with humor.

23. Humor sets free

Untie him and let him go (Jn 11:1-44).

The story is the raising of Lazarus, the brother of Martha and Mary, at Bethany, near Jerusalem (somewhere in March, in the year 30 A.D.). John's narrative is a jewel of simplicity and psychology. It is the work of an artist who has been an eye-witness.

Martha is the lady of the house, busy and preoccupied, worried and disturbed (no. 28). Mary is the one who anoints the Lord with perfume and wipes off his feet with her hair, while her sister is busy with the serving (Jn 12:2).

When Jesus arrives in the vicinity of the village, Martha goes out to meet him. Mary stays sitting at home (v. 20). Martha is constantly at work, active, always in motion. Mary remains seated, takes her time; but one must be careful not to misjudge her: there is a whole hidden dynamism in this "contemplative" soul: when she acts, she acts decisively. It is she who spread the precious ointment on Jesus so liberally as to perfume the entire house (Jn 12:3).

Martha comes to tell her sister that the Master is there, just outside the village, asking for her. Mary jumps up and runs to meet him, "in haste." Mary makes no move towards our Lord, but when he gives her a sign, she acts in a prompt and decisive manner. We must note that the people did not follow Martha, but "when the Jews who were with her in the house, consoling her, saw Mary rise quickly and go out, they followed her, supposing that she was going to the tomb to weep there" (v. 31). It is Mary who is the more popular of the two.

The two sisters had frequently spoken of Jesus during their brother's sickness, and during the four days after his death. They kept saying: "If only Jesus had been here, he would have healed Lazarus . . . If he had been here, Lazarus would not have died . . ." This is what Martha hastens to tell Jesus, and this is what Mary repeats, in her turn: "Lord, if you had been here, my brother would not have died." She begins to weep. "When Jesus saw her, he was deeply moved in spirit and troubled, and he said, 'Where have you laid him?' And Jesus wept" (v. 35).

"Then Jesus, deeply moved again, came to the tomb; it was a cave, and a stone lay upon it. Jesus said, 'Take away the stone.' Martha (it was not Mary, who never would have hesitated at any of Jesus' orders) says, 'Lord, by this time there will be an odor, for he has been dead four days.' 'Did I not say that if you would believe you would see the glory of God?' So they took away the stone."

Then Jesus cried out in a loud voice, "Lazarus, come out." The dead man came out, his hands and feet bound with bandages, and his face wrapped with a cloth, looking like a mummy. How can we describe the reaction, the amazement of the eye-witnesses, Martha and Mary, the disciples, the crowd of people? They are all struck speechless. There is only one person who has the presence of mind to realize that poor Lazarus, all bound up as he is, needs some help: "Unbind him, and let him go." Let him go from his bonds: he cannot walk that way. It is the same person who earlier said, at the occasion of raising the daughter of Jairus, "Give her something to eat" (no. 22). Humor frees us from many bonds.

> Lord, I often have hands and feet tied up.
> I do not know what to do: I am dead.
> Lord, wake me up . . .
> Bring me out of the tomb.

23b. Resurrection and revivification

The Gospel recounts three raisings from the dead that Jesus performed, without mentioning that of Jesus himself: The raising of Lazarus (no. 23), the daughter of Jairus (no. 22), and the son of the widow of Naim (no. 21). In these three cases it would be more exact to speak of a "revivification" or a "re-animation" than of a resurrection properly so-called. We should more accurately reserve the term "resurrection" for the Resurrection of Jesus, and our own resurrection in the image of Jesus'.

It is true that in the case of both resurrection and revivification, the point of departure is one and the same: first there is the duly verified fact of death, supported by several witnesses. In the case of Lazarus, Martha says "there is already an odor" (Jn 11:39).

But all the points of similarity, no matter how many we find, all entail one essential difference. In both cases the body and soul are reunited, and the person is once again alive. Still, in the resurrection properly so called, that of Jesus (the first-fruits of those who have been raised) (no. 14), the body is transformed; it is in a state quite different from the former mortal body. The body is endowed with new qualities, new dynamism which frees it from the limitations of matter. St. Paul (1 Cor 15:44) calls it "a spiritual body," because in this state the union between flesh and spirit is perfect.

In the case of "revivification," what is involved is a pure and simple return to the bodily state with which we are familiar, with all its dependency and all its limitations. Thus Lazarus, the daughter of Jairus, and the son of the widow of Naim, did not have a "spiritualized" body when they came back to life on earth. Thus they needed, like Lazarus, to be untied, or, like the daughter of Jairus, to have something to eat.

If the reader is interested in pursuing this subject, he might read the fifth chapter of the first letter of St. Paul to the Corinthians, which answers the question "how are the dead brought back to life? with what kind of body do they return?" (v. 35). The first Christians asked the same questions that we are asking in the twentieth century. We might also reflect on the state of Jesus' body as described in his apparitions (cf. nos. 55, 56, 57, 58). It is through the dynamism of the resurrected Jesus, and in the image of his glorious body, that all the dead will one day rise again: "But our commonwealth is in heaven, and from it we await a Savior, the Lord Jesus Christ, who will change our lowly bodies to be like his glorified body, by the power which enables him even to subject all things to himself" (Ph 3:20).

In my opinion, there would be little point in asking these three people about their experiences between the time of their death and their revivification: most probably they would remember absolutely nothing, just like people who awaken from a sound sleep. In this connection we might recall Jesus' insistence on sleep (Jn 11:11; Lk 8:52). This is perhaps one of the examples of Jesus' double meaning (cf. no. 5).

There is nothing to be gained from indulging in the

sick humor of a certain doctor of Canon Law who posed
the question of whether Lazarus, upon his return to life,
had a right to reclaim from his wife and his sister all
the property that he had bequeathed to them; the answer to this question requires a distinction between the
rigor of the law and the principles of equity.

Finally we must note that the "resurrections" performed by Jesus are signs and prefigurations of the true
resurrection that is to come: "Whoever lives and believes
in me will not ever die . . . I am the resurrection" (Jn
11:25); "I will raise him up on the last day" (Jn 6:44).

24. Humor finds the answer for a haughty Pharisee

You have judged well (Lk 7:36-50).

Jesus has been invited to dinner at the house of
Simon, a Pharisee. We are in a village in Galilee (probably in September or October of the year 28). A third
person makes her arrival, a woman, "a woman of the
city, who was a sinner." She had already seen Jesus.
Mixed in with the crowd, she had no doubt heard him
explain his teaching on repentance and forgiveness. The
gentleness with which she had seen him welcome sinners
had touched her heart. She thus makes her way into the
banquet hall, where the guests were reclining along the
outside of a horseshoe-shaped table (no. 47). She makes
her way between the guests and the wall of the room,
coming to a stop behind Jesus, who is reclining on the
couch with his feet facing out.

Knowing full well that he will not reject her, she
bursts into a flood of tears, brought on by her joy at his
presence as well as her repentance for her sins. Her
tears fall on Jesus' feet which, in keeping with the
custom of his people, are bare. To dry them, she makes
use of her beautiful long hair. Then she began to cover

them with kisses. Finally, breaking the neck of an alabaster flask of ointment which she had brought with her, she spreads the sweet perfume upon the feet just washed by her tears. She says not a single word: her actions are a sufficient expression of the depth of feeling within.

Seeing all this, the Pharisee who had invited Jesus to dinner began to say within himself: "If this man were a prophet, he would have known who and what sort of woman this is who is touching him, for she is a sinner." But Jesus turned to him and said in answer: "Simon, I have something to say to you." He answered, "What is it, Teacher?" "A certain creditor had two debtors; one owed 500 denarii (about $180), the other 50. When they could not pay, he forgave them both. Now which of them will love him more?" Simon is beginning to suspect a trap, but he answers, "The one, I suppose, to whom he forgave more."

Jesus said to him, "You have judged rightly." He approves the Pharisee's answer, but then he invites him to carry his logic one step further and apply it to the present situation: "you have judged rightly" but now continue to judge, between your hospitality and the hospitality offered by this woman. "I entered your house, you gave me no water for my feet, but she has wet my feet with her tears and wiped them with her hair. You gave me no kiss, but from the time I came in she has not ceased to kiss my feet. You did not anoint my head with oil, but she has anointed my feet with ointment."

Then comes the application. First he turns to the woman, "Therefore, I tell you, her sins, which are many, are forgiven, for she loved much." And the application to Simon, "But he who is forgiven little, loves little."

Finally he says to the woman, "Your sins are forgiven." Those who were at table with him began to ask each other, "Who is this, who even forgives sins?" Jesus makes no attempt to establish his credentials for forgiving sins: he has already done this before (no. 9). He turns to the woman instead: "Your faith has saved you; go in peace."

> Lord, you do not want our condemnations
>   against our brothers and our sisters.
> You hate sin, but you love the sinner.
> Give us a heart like yours,
>   full of love and of humor.

25. Humor is too strong for the crumbling old forms

New wine and old wine skins (Mt 9:17).

Jesus uses two very familiar and picturesque comparisons: old clothes and old "jugs." First a lesson about mending clothes: Every good housewife, in Palestine and everywhere else, knows how to prolong the life of an old garment by sewing on a patch, but never a patch of new cloth, because it could easily pull out and damage the old garment still further. Bottles made out of goatskin are, even today, frequently used in Palestine to carry and preserve all kinds of liquids: water, milk, oil, wine. But if these wineskins get too old, they let the liquid escape.

The "new patch" and the "new wine" (just like the "gate" and the "way" in Mt 7:13-14) refer to the "new spirit" of the Gospel which cannot be infused into the old Mosaic Law, which had degenerated into Pharisaism. The Pharisees did not see the law as a whole, as having a spirit, but rather in its individual concrete applications, the rigorously. fixed observances that held a grip on every circumstance of life. They had established 638 precepts. What the Savior is telling them is that the new spirit of the Gospel is not compatible with minutiae of this sort: it would be a serious distortion to attempt any adaptation. The apostles do not fast after the manner of the Pharisees. They do not observe the sabbath the way the Pharisees understand it. They do not practice all their petty and meaningless ablutions.

The "old wine jugs" (and there are always some of them around) are the Scribes, the Pharisees, the doctors of the Law, the educated intellectuals, brilliant and facile minds, clear in their ideas but narrow in their judgment, legalistic, and for them the gospel is "too strong": "These words are too strong. Who can hear them!" (Jn 6:60).

The "new wine jugs" are the sinners of Galilee, uneducated and long-haired, the publicans like Matthew and Zachaeus, the prostitutes like Mary Magdalene, the little people, the man on the street: "I thank thee, Father, Lord of heaven and earth, that thou has hidden these things from the wise and understanding and revealed them to babes" (Mt 11:25).

The new wine of the Gospel is to be put into new wineskins, wineskins that are perfectly adapted to it, and then everything will work out well. Christianity will be the new garment which is perfectly fitted to the new, reborn human being. It cannot be simply a patch sewn onto the Judaism of the Pharisees; its spirit is too new to stick to the old forms.

No new patches for an old garment. No new wine for old wineskins.

Lord, I am afraid
    of being an old wineskin and an old garment.
Give me the grace to be a new wineskin and a
    new garment.
Help me to renew myself,
    to renew others,
    with love and with humor.

26. Humor gives its sign

The sign of Jonah (Mt 12:38-42).

"This evil and adulterous generation seeks for a sign."
The scribes and Pharisees (the theologians and intellectuals of those days) are demanding a sign from Jesus.
It is not the first time. After the daring and forceful ex-
pulsion of the money-changers from the Temple, accompanied by the shouts and laughter of the crowd whom
they had too often exploited, the leaders of the people
and the Temple, suspicious and jealous accomplices of
the merchants, attempt to save face by saying, "What
sign do you give us for acting like this?" (Jn 2:18).
Jesus has already performed a great number of signs:
he has restored sight to the blind, made crippled people
walk again, made dumb people speak again, multiplied
the loaves and the fishes—but all this had been done for
the simple people, idlers and day-dreamers, naive and
credulous people, in a word, for the common people.
There was not a single member of the upper classes
who believed in him (Jn 7:48-49). Let him now work
a miracle "upon request," in front of people who were
informed, expert, and under conditions that were scien-
tifically controlled—"And we will believe in him." Jesus
is well aware of what motivates such people; he knows
that their invitation, sincere though it may sound, is
really only a hypocritical challenge, a statement of their
systematic opposition.
Jesus never lets himself become involved in these
ridiculous "laboratory" miracles, these miracles of pure
and simple ostentation, any more than he gave in to the
devil's challenge and invitation to cast himself down
from the pinnacle of the Temple (Mt 4:6), any more
than he was to give in to the invitation proposed at
Herod's vain and curious court (Lk 23:8). The malicious

curiosity of the scribes is equally a waste of their time and effort. A miracle will be given to them one day, indeed, and a very striking one at that. But this will not be the kind of miracle these people had hoped to see. Their hypocrisy is always open to Jesus' direct attacks. The occasion is simply too favorable for him to pass it by. "You are an evil and adulterous generation."

At the same time, Jesus seizes upon this opportunity to make the very first and very striking promise of his resurrection. The sign he gives is the "sign of Jonah": "Just as Jonah was three days and three nights in the belly of the whale, so will the Son of Man be three days and three nights in the heart of the earth." For his Jewish audience, the expression "three days and three nights" would not be understood to mean 72 hours, as it would for us, latter-day Cartesians, mathematicians in the IBM era. For them, a fraction of the day counted as a whole day, and the same manner of expression applied to the month and year as well.

On a certain Thursday in the future, a day which we call Holy Thursday, the chief priests and scribes and elders of the people will once again, in mockery, demand a final sign from Jesus on the cross: "Let the Christ, the king of Israel, come down now from the cross, so that we may see and believe" (Mk 15:32). They will not even suspect it when "the sign of Jonah" has actually begun, when, from this Thursday until the third day following, the Son of Man will be in the heart of the earth. They will not even suspect what is destined to happen on that third day, the first Sunday of the Christian era. They will completely miss the meaning of this "sign" that Humor has given them.

Lord, you give us a sign.
Give us the grace not to miss

"your" signs day after day.
Give us the grace to open our eyes.

27. Humor explains the Law

Who has touched my robe? (Mk 5:25-34).

"There was a woman who had had a flow of blood for
twelve years, and who had suffered much under many
physicians, and had spent all that she had, and was no
better but rather grew worse. She had heard the reports
about Jesus, and came up behind him in the crowd and
touched his garment." St. Luke (8:43), in recounting
this same incident, omits the remark that "she was no
better but rather grew worse." St. Luke was, after all,
a doctor himself (Col 4:14): he certainly did not want to
report anything that would embarrass his profession.

But Mark, in a more concrete vein, continues the
narrative: "Immediately the hemorrhage ceased; and
she felt in her body that she was healed of her disease.
Jesus, perceiving in himself that power had gone forth
from him, immediately turned about in the crowd, and
said, 'Who touched my garment?'" His disciples are
astounded at the question: "You see the crowd pressing
around you, and yet you say, 'Who touched me?'"

But Jesus looked around him to discover who had
touched him. The evangelist describes the woman as
coming "in fear and trembling": the reason was that
this sickness, in addition to its humiliating nature, put
her in a state of legal uncleanness, making her a source
of contamination for everyone who touched her (Lv 15:
25-27).

Why should Jesus have demanded this woman to
make public her furtive gesture? If the Master asks her
something like this, it is not for himself that he asks,
and certainly not to humiliate the poor woman. It is to

explain about faith and miracles. If she has been cured, this is not the result of her having partaken in some strange power that radiates from Jesus and produces miracles; rather it is because Jesus himself wanted to perform this wonder. What is more, he performed it by reason of her faith in his supernatural power, a faith which she displayed publicly by touching the hem of his garment. There is a message here that Jesus means to stress, both for this woman and for everybody in the crowd around him.

"Daughter, your faith has made you well; go in peace, and be healed of your disease." You have been healed and you will remain healed. You have shown a great faith. I consider you as my child, my daughter. Humor glorifies faith.

Lord, teach me to believe.
Faith is not this or that.
Faith is you, always you.
Lord, glorify my faith.

28. Humor is satisfied with just a little, but this little is essential

Martha, you are anxious and troubled about many things (Lk 10:38-42).

This event takes place at Bethany, near Jerusalem (sometime near November of the year 29). Jesus has been received into a home whose mistress seems to be Martha, for it is said that she receives him "in her house" (v. 38). She has a sister named Mary. Their two temperaments are entirely opposite (no. 23). Mary sits down at the Lord's feet: she is listening to his words. Martha, on the other hand, is all taken up with the many tasks of preparation. She is constantly making signs to her "do-nothing" of a sister who is leaving all the work to her. But Mary cannot be budged; she sees and hears nothing but Jesus.

Finally, Martha can contain herself no longer. She addresses her complaint to Jesus, not to Mary; for Mary does not want to listen to her. In an impatient and even indignant tone she cries out, "Lord, do you not care that my sister has left me to serve alone? Tell her then to help me." The scene is strikingly presented. And what familiarity with Jesus! To a certain degree, she is right. Jesus has just arrived with a company of twelve hearty appetites. It is her responsibility to set a meal worthy of the house's reputation. She certainly needs Mary's help.

From this point of view, we might well be surprised at Jesus' answer: "Martha, Martha, you are anxious and troubled about many things; one thing is needful. Mary has chosen the good portion, which shall not be taken away from her." It seems that Jesus is always coming to the defense of Mary. Later he is to defend her against Judas, when she "wastes" a whole pound of very expensive nard, by pouring it over Jesus' feet (Jn 12:7).

Here once again we must recognize a double meaning in Jesus' words (no. 5). The surface meaning is that Jesus is telling Martha that she is doing too much. She wants to prepare a sumptuous repast for them, and this makes her nervous, impatient. All that he and his companions require is just a little something to sustain them: a cup of coffee or a glass of cold water, perhaps a biscuit or a piece of bread. She would do better to come and sit at his feet, together with her sister Mary, and listen to him: he does not pass by that way very often.

But at the same time, a much more profound meaning is being conveyed: "Mary has chosen the good portion." We must take advantage of Jesus while he is here, and not be distracted by our "legitimate" preoccupations. We must not lose even a single one of his words. Thus we see a deeper development and explanation of the opposition between "many things" and "one single thing." From the point of view of the dinner, we pass on to the perspective of life with Christ: We must get rid of many things, good in themselves, in order to embrace one single thing, which is the only thing truly necessary, the essential thing: to be with him.

In my personal experience, I have been led to a very "vital" understanding of this incident at Bethany in the course of my meetings with lay people. We all get together once a month, about thirty of us (men and women from every walk of life): the members of the group take turns playing host in their living rooms. Our meetings are a communal reflection on some passage from the Gospels. After the meeting, there is always something to eat. And this is where Mary gets the better of Martha. We have made it a general rule, and stuck to it, that the refreshments should be limited to something simple to drink (coffee, tea, light beverage) and maybe a few cookies. Nothing elaborate: no cake, no pie, no complicated sandwiches. Our intention was that the host should not need to be distracted and occupied about many things, since we only need just a little bit. We would rather have her sitting together with us, with nothing to distract her in any way, sharing in the Word. Otherwise, the refreshments would soon turn into a competition between one house and the other, and the fruits of our encounter with the Lord would all be lost. Humor is satisfied with very little, but this very little is essential.

Lord, often I am disturbed
    and troubled about many things.
Make me concentrate upon what is essential:
    to be together with you and with my brethren,
    with love and with humor.

29. Humor avoids self-seeking quarrels

"Who made me a judge or divider over you?"
(Lk 12:13-21).

We are in Judea (around November of the year 29). Someone in the crowd has just said, "Teacher, bid my brother divide the inheritance with me." It is a plaintiff addressing himself to Jesus as he would be a rabbi whose authority was widely recognized. Convinced that the law is on his side, he asks the Master to intervene in the disputation over an inheritance, without any attempt to explain the reasons which would justify his request. We might presume that his elder brother, instead of following the law set down in Deuteronomy (21:17), which awarded two-thirds of the inheritance to him, had instead kept the entire amount, without bothering to give his younger brother the part which was legally his.

Jesus declines this request for his intervention: "Man, who made me a judge or divider over you?" It is not his business to regulate material things, where all too frequently there is an encounter and clash between two opposing egotisms. If Jesus speaks of wealth, it is not in order to intervene in the process of its disposition, a matter for law and society, but rather to make clear how it ought to be used, to explain the duties incumbent upon those who possess it. If he is judge, it is not of temporal affairs, but rather of men who live within a framework of time. His role is to lead all mankind towards love.

Still, the question that has been asked must not prove entirely useless. It serves to introduce an instruction on the subject of wealth, aimed particularly at the two brothers who are in conflict: "Take heed, and beware of all covetousness." What both the elder and younger brother actually need is conversion, a chance to learn how to detach themselves from their wealth. Jesus has enough sense of humor not to take sides, for the avarice of the one against the avarice of the other.

In the course of human history, with all its quarrels and all its wars, people have frequently attempted to get Jesus on their side, to claim him for their champion, to enroll him in their military force. We try to involve Jesus in all sorts of ambiguities. The very same thing is happening even today. In a rather recent book (Frère Hilaire, **Humor en Eglise,** Editions Paulines, 1971) an attempt is made to warn a community of nuns against this danger, through the methodology of questions and answers. The world asks a question: "In your convent, is it customary to be opposed to politics? Can I take the habit without leaving the party?" The nun receives this advice: "Do not look for anything to say. Is it not enough merely to laugh?" Some "Christians" put this question: "Are you progressive? I am an integrist." The same advice: "Do not look for anything to say. Is it not enough merely to laugh?"

> If anybody involves you in the work
>   of making the Church a democracy,
>   of making the Kingdom a socialist state,
>   of making the Gospel something political,
> Do not look for anything to say.
> Is it not enough merely to laugh?

30. Humor transforms insult into kindness

It is not fair to take the children's bread and throw it to the dogs (Mt 15:21-28).

Jesus withdrew into the region of Tyre and Sidon (around the end of June in the year 29). A woman, a Canaanite, cried out to him, "Have mercy on me, oh

Lord, Son of David; my daughter is severely possessed by a demon." In answer he told her, "It is not fair to take the children's bread and throw it to the dogs."

At first hearing. Jesus' answer is surprising: we are strongly tempted to see his reference to "dogs" as an insult, as a statement in very bad taste. I had the personal experience, at Hebron, near the tomb of Abraham, of having a Mohammedan cross my path and address me with what was for him the supreme insult: "Kelb!", that is "dog," and spit on the ground. To his thinking, this was the worst insult that one faithful to Allah could possibly address to a Christian "infidel" who did not admit to Mohammed. In our own society, the epithet would more likely be developed into "son of a bitch." In Jesus' time, the Jews considered themselves (and actually were) the People of God, the children of Yahweh, and looked down upon the pagans as "children of fornication," born of an unknown father. That is the point of reference when they tell Jesus, "We were not born of fornication; we have one Father, even God" (Jn 8:41).

In response to the Canaanite woman, Jesus is certainly making some reference to the attitudes of his compatriots, a reference which is at least to some degree insulting for the woman. But it is precisely here that Jesus' supreme art is so much to be admired: in his mouth, the insulting word turns into what is rather a pleasant and benevolent exchange of banter. Once when I was in conference with some English-speaking confreres, I chanced to refer to them, in jest, as **"maudits anglais,"** whereupon they promptly retorted "damn Frenchman." We were playing with insults. Thus, reflecting upon the context of the Gospel narrative, we cannot help but note the adjective and the diminutive, "little" dog: this is already enough to soften the meaning and make it something affectionate. I find it easy to envision the sparkle of wit in Jesus' eyes, the pleasant smile spreading across his lips, and I can hear the benevolent tone with which he invites the woman's response.

Only humor can understand Humor. Only love can understand Love. The Canaanite woman, without either humor or love, would have remained cold and distant, would have felt insulted, for, so far as the words themselves were concerned, he had called her "a bitch"; that was the verbal logic of his statement. But instead she understands that Jesus is jesting with her, without in any way offering her the least insult. It is up to her to discover the proper response, the proper bearing, humor, and love. She decides to play the game with him, taking him up in his own words: "Yes, Lord." Then she plays upon his use of the words "little dogs," using them as the basis of her further argument: "Yet even the little dogs eat the crumbs that fall from their master's table."

A truly admirable response, quite to the point, and very telling: "The crumbs": all that I am asking for is just a crumb of your power and your love; "their master's table": she accepts the fact that salvation comes from the Jews (Jn 4:22); "little dogs": yes, I am a little dog, but I too have a right to eat. Jesus realizes all this and expresses his admiration: "Oh woman, great is your faith." On more than one occasion Jesus will encounter a similar faith among the pagans, for example, in the case of the centurion: "When Jesus heard him, he marveled, and said to those who followed him, 'Truly, I say to you, not even in Israel have I found such faith'" (Mt 8:10).

The story ends as we might well expect: "And her daughter was healed at the very moment," a moment of humor and love on the part of Jesus and the Canaanite woman alike.

31. Humor stays with the "little ones"

Zachaeus, come down quickly! (Lk 19:1-10).

Jesus is on his way to Jerusalem. He is going by way of Jericho, near the Jordan (March, A.D. 30). A large crowd is following him, completely surrounding him. Along the road there is a man named Zachaeus; he was a chief tax-collector, and very rich. He had wanted very much to see Jesus. He tries to make his way through the thick press of the crowd, but it is to no avail; he cannot see anything, "on account of the crowd, because he was small of stature." With a true Oriental simplicity and determination, he runs on ahead of the procession. Without further thought, and without fearing that his position as a wealthy citizen will be subjected to any kind of ridicule, he climbs up into a tree, like a young boy, and waits for Jesus to pass by underneath.

When Jesus arrives alongside the tree, he raises his eyes, sparkling with humor, and cries out, "Zachaeus, come down quickly; for I must stay at your house today." All Zachaeus wanted was to see Jesus: and now Jesus had invited himself to stay with him. The little man hastens down from the tree, runs to meet Jesus, escorts him with great pride, and receives him with joy into his home.

But not everybody is pleased with the way things have worked out. The pious souls are telling each other that if Jesus was serious and religious-minded, he could have chosen better; for example, he might have chosen the house of a scribe who was well versed in the Scriptures, or the house of a priest who was faithful to the temple worship. But just think, "he has gone in to be the guest of a man who is a sinner." For these legalistically pure people, to be a publican is to be a sinner (cf.

Lk 18:9-14). The reason is that the publicans practiced a hated profession; they were the tax-collectors, in the service of the Roman Empire, of the "establishment," the Romans.

Peoples' attitudes seldom vary with respect to taxes.[1] In Palestine, the words publican, thief, and sinner had all become synonymous, as we frequently note in the Gospels (cf. Mt 9:10). To frequent these people meant to encourage injustice, to favor the enemy, the Roman Empire, etc. What is more, for the Pharisees, it involved the incurring of all kinds of legal uncleanness.

Zachaeus is not unaware of what people think of him, nor of what they are saying about the master. He stands up to his full stature, face to face with Jesus, and says, "Behold, Lord, the half of my goods I give to the poor; and if I have defrauded anyone of anything, I restore it fourfold." "Here I am": this is the fundamental attitude of conversion. It is the gift of oneself to accomplish the will of God (Lk 1:38). Zachaeus has heard a report of what Jesus thinks about wealth, that fortunes are to be used to help the poor, and thus he is willing to give one half of his. He is well aware of having committed some injustices in an unfair system of tax collection: he will make generous amends. His is a con-

---

1. It must be pointed out that the Roman Emperor made use of rather original methods for collecting his taxes: he used to let out a contract for their collection. This means that, in the case of Palestine, for example, Pilate the procurator was taxed a certain sum for the whole province of Judea. Let us suppose that for the year in question Pilate owed the Emperor Tiberius (Lk 3:1) the sum of ten million denarii. Provided that he managed to pay this sum, no one asked him any questions and his position was secure. Pilate accordingly would turn to the chief tax collectors of the individual cities (Jerusalem, Jericho, etc.), villages (Bethany, Emmaus, etc.), and subcontract to them the collection for their territory, demanding 100,000 denarii from one, 50,000 from another, according to what the population could produce. The result would amount to, let us say, fifteen million, ten of which had to be passed on to Rome. The abuses of the system were known and tolerated at Rome. What is more, Tiberius made it a practice to leave the

version not in word only, but in actual deed, an authentic conversion.

Jesus, too, has something to say: "Today salvation has come to this house, since he also is a son of Abraham. For the Son of Man came to seek and to save the lost." For Jesus, salvation is available to all men of good will, even if they are tax-collectors.

Jesus, you want to stay with me.
Make me come down quickly,
   to receive you with joy.
I do not dare to say
   that I will give half of what I have,
   that I will repay fourfold.
But you help me to do what Zachaeus did.

---

same procurators in power for several years so that they would amass considerable wealth, and grow less greedy as the years went by, like the dog and the ticks in Aesop's fable.

The example began from the very top and it was imitated all down the line. And thus Zachaeus, the chief tax collector for the territory of Jericho, had to supply Pilate with, let us say, 100,000 denarii—Jericho being a very rich agricultural district. If Zachaeus followed the established custom, he would entrust the collection to various subalterns among the Pharisees, in such a manner as to end up collecting about 150,000 denarii. And the publicans (Matthew was one of them for the district of Capernaum) carried the practice one step further. The multiplication was a geometric progression. It is easy to understand why John the Baptist preached to the publicans that they should not demand more than what was fixed by law, and why he told the soldiers not to rob anyone by violence or false accusation and to be content with their wages (cf. Lk 3; 12-14).

IV.

JESUS' HUMOR WITH HIS DISCIPLES

Constantly around Jesus is a group of twelve apostles, chosen by him. He is preparing them for a work of universal and eternal significance. But they are not without their faults, they have little understanding for the things of God, they are petty, vain, ambitious. Christ's teaching, here too, is a work of love, and frequently of humor (nos. 32-45).

32. Humor takes a long view

When you were under the fig tree, I saw you (Jn 1:45-51).

I have always wondered what Nathanael was doing under the fig tree. When I finally get to heaven, through the mercy of Jesus, what I plan to do, immediately after saying hello to the Blessed Trinity and the Blessed Virgin, is to call Nathanael on the intercom, and ask him what he was doing there, under that fig tree, sometime around March in the year 28. When I first started reading the Gospels, I used to find many of these trailing references, which seemed to lead nowhere, to have no purpose. Then, upon reflection, I came to see them as a proof of the evangelist's truthfulness. A novelist would not leave his reader's curiosity unsatisfied, or he would not be a very good novelist. But the sacred writers are not writing to satisfy my curiosity: they are trying to lead me to Jesus. And so, devil take my curiosity!

Always, I can see humor in these words of Jesus:

"When you were under the fig tree, I saw you." If Jesus saw him, it was not through the glass of a binoculars: there was no such invention in those days. And still, our Lord has a long view, which can see at great distance. In fact, he also has an x-ray to delve into the secrets of men's hearts: "He knows what there is in a man" (no. 7). He knows that the Samaritan woman has had five husbands (no. 19). He knows when his disciples are murmuring behind his back (no. 39); he knows when he will die (Jn 13:1); who will betray him (no. 47); when somebody wants to ask him something, he is aware of the fact (Jn 16:19). He knows that Peter will deny him (no. 48); that the apostles will abandon him (Jn 16:32). He knows everything that is going to happen to him (Jn 18:4). He knows how Peter is going to die (no. 60). And as for me, I know now, thanks to the Gospel, that Jesus saw Nathanael under the fig tree.

I have a further question to ask Nathanael. I would like to know how it was possible for him to be converted so quickly: "Rabbi, you are the Son of God. You are the King of Israel." Even Jesus found this a little surprising: "Because I said to you, I saw you under the fig tree, do you believe? You shall see greater things than these." And what is it that he shall see? "Truly, truly, I say to you, you will see heaven opened, and the angels of God ascending and descending upon the Son of Man." Even I would believe if I were to see all that.

But Nathanael believed without seeing anything of this. Perhaps the reason is, as Jesus says, that he was "an Israelite indeed, in whom there is no guile," that is, "a good Jew." And still, Nathanael had expressed contempt for the city of Nazareth, though he himself came from the neighboring village of Cana: "Can anything good come out of Nazareth?" Jesus makes no allusion to this disparaging remark addressed to his native city:

his sense of humor was big enough to understand the petty rivalries between one village and another.

> Lord, you see me;
>> you know my thoughts before I speak them.
>> You know my actions before I do them.
> You are marvelous.
> I too am marvelous.
> Lord, look upon me all you want,
>> with love and with humor.

33. Humor teaches a theologian

Are you a teacher of Israel, and yet you do not understand this? (Jn 3:1-21).

Nicodemus is a Pharisee, one of the important Jews, a "teacher of Israel," an "expert" in the Law and in the teaching; we would call him a doctor of theology. He considers Jesus as a great rabbi, a master, a doctor of divine sciences. He comes by night, during one of Jesus' sojourns in Jerusalem, around the time of the Passover (A.D. 28). He has been much impressed by Jesus' preaching and miracles: "Rabbi, we know that you are a teacher come from God; for no one can do these signs that you do, unless God is with him."

Jesus knows how to suit his language to his audience. Speaking to the people, he likes to tell stories, the parables (cf. Mt 13). In conversation with the Samaritan woman at the well of Jacob, he speaks of living water (no. 18). Here, this night, he is dealing with an educated man. Still, the approach of the theologian can be too exclusively intellectual, not "existential" enough. It is not enough to think about God; it is also necessary to live God, and this demands a rebirth of the entire person:

"Truly, I say to you, unless one is born anew, he cannot see the kingdom of God." Jesus is alluding to baptism, and its gift of a new being, to live in God.

Despite all his theology, Nicodemus cannot understand any more than the apostles or the Samaritan woman. His reasoning is "according to the flesh." His answer is couched in the thinking of this earth, and hence it quite misses the point: "How can a man be born when he is old? Can he enter a second time into his mother's womb and be born?" Nicodemus has set himself up as a judge of the Savior's teaching. But he is going to be reduced, instead, to the condition of an ignorant apprentice.

Jesus does not allude to this "teacher's" inability to understand. Instead, he sets forth a profound teaching on the subject of baptism, realizing that Nicodemus will think about it and understand it later on. First of all, Jesus insists upon the necessity of baptism. "Truly, truly, I say to you, unless one is born of water and the Spirit, he cannot enter the kingdom of God." Next, he explains the activity of the Holy Spirit: "That which is born of the flesh is flesh, and that which is born of the Spirit is spirit."

Nicodemus still cannot understand. "How can this be?" What he wants to understand is the technique of this baptism and the activity of the Spirit. Whenever we refuse to admit the substance of what the Master says, we fall back upon technique and methodology, in an effort to appear intelligent. It is here that Jesus shows his humor, and perhaps his irony as well, after having spent the entire night putting up with the intellectual pretentions of this traditionally educated Pharisee: "Are you a teacher of Israel, and yet you do not understand this?" You have your doctorate in theology and you do not even know the ABC's of life in God.

Jesus continues, nonetheless, to instruct Nicodemus,

knowing that the seed is falling on ground that still bears the mark of pharisaical thorns, but ground that is good enough to produce the proper fruit some day in the future (cf. Mt 13:3-28). To begin with, Jesus asserts the authority of his teaching: "We speak of what we know, and bear witness to what we have seen; but you do not receive our testimony." Then he gives Nicodemus a warning which is addressed to all the Pharisees: "Men loved darkness rather than light, because their deeds were evil." Finally, he congratulates him and encourages this man who came to him "by night." "He who does what is true comes to the light, that it may be clearly seen that his deeds have been wrought in God."

Nicodemus was to remain faithful to Jesus. The day would come when the chief priests and Pharisees send out soldiers to arrest our Savior (Jn 7:48-52). Mixing in with the crowd, they listen to Jesus instead, and forget that they are to arrest him. They return filled with enthusiasm: "No one has ever spoken like this man." The Pharisees answer them, "Have you too let yourselves be taken in by his words!" It is at this point that Nicodemus intervenes: "Does our law judge a man without first giving him a hearing and learning what he does?" They retort, "Are you from Galilee too? Search, and you will see that no prophet is to rise from Galilee." Their theology is clear, to the point of being simplistic. Nothing good can come from Galilee (cf. Jn 1:46). Their recommendation is brief and peremptory: "Search." Everyone who has conducted such a search, all the "well-informed" circles, that is, all of us,—we know what to think. Their scorn is a threat in itself, an act of intimidation by group solidarity: are you too a Galilean? If you do not think as we do, then beware.

As a matter of fact, Nicodemus is indeed "a Galilean," but still a very hidden one. He withdraws in silence, for he has not yet found the courage to stand up to his colleagues: "Many even of the authorities believed in him, but for fear of the Pharisees they did not confess it, lest they should be put out of the synagogue: for they loved the praise of men more than the praise of God" (Jn 12:42). Even today, when the ideas of "thinking people," the opinion of the "well-informed groups" is not favorable to "the Galilean," and can only look down on the "ignorant rabble" who actually follow him—it is not the time to expect a journalist, an editor, a commentator, a professor to "declare for him." There is always the danger of being excluded from one's "group," one's "clique." It is still more profitable to "love the praises of men more than the praise of God."

On the evening of Jesus' death, Nicodemus will declare himself boldly, in company with Joseph of Arimathea, another man who is "a disciple of Jesus, but secretly, out of fear of the Jews" (Jn 19:38). They will obtain Pilate's authorization to bury the body of Jesus.

> Lord Jesus,
>   to know, that is something,
>   but to live, that is more,
>   to declare oneself, that is courage.
> My clear ideas
>   are often darkness,
>   satisfaction without action.
> It is Love and Humor
>   which bring light,
>   which make witness.

34. Humor makes things grow, by cutting down

He must increase, but I must decrease (Jn 3:30).

Everyone who draws near to Jesus seems to acquire

something of his humor. Even John the Baptist, with his uncouth appearance, clad in animal skins, eating locusts and wild honey (Mt 3:4), seems to show some of his humor: "He must increase, but I must decrease." In the circumstances what the Baptist means to say is that Jesus is destined to grow in his reputation and that many of the precursor's disciples will follow the Messiah (Jn 1:37); as a result, John himself will diminish in popularity and his disciples will diminish in number.

At the same time, might we not find here another level of prophetic meaning, inspired by the humor of the Spirit, who speaks with such purpose and wealth of meaning through his prophets? (Lk 12:12). Jesus will indeed grow in stature, raised up physically upon the cross (cf. Jn 12:32). John the Baptist will grow less physically, his head cut off (Mt 14:11).

> Lord, in order for you to grow big in me,
>   let my egotism grow smaller.
> Full development
>   comes through renunciation,
>   life through death.
> Give me the grace
>   to understand you,
>   and to live from you.

35. Humor gives an invitation to fish

I will make you fishers of men (Mt 4:18-22).

Everyone who likes to fish can appreciate the humor of this invitation on the part of Jesus. It is the definitive calling of the first four apostles (May, A.D. 28). The four fishermen are all colleagues, and they own two boats: one belongs to the two brothers Simon and Andrew, the other to Zebedee, father of James and John. They were fishing in the Lake of Genesareth. Their home port was the city of Capernaum.

Before calling them, Jesus has made use of Peter's boat (Lk 5:1-7). He tells them now, "Put out into the deep and let down your nets for a catch." Everyone knows how easy it is to influence a fisherman. Simply walk up to one standing on the shore and tell him, "A little bit over to the left, that's where the trout are," and just watch what happens. Now Simon is a fisherman: "Master, we toiled all night and took nothing. But at your word I will let down the nets." The catch was amazing. The nets were actually breaking because of the great quantity of fish. They had to call to Zebedee's boat for help, and they filled both boats.

Whenever we happen to meet a fellow fishing enthusiast, we know that we have met a friend. But this Fisherman invites his friends to go fishing for men. He could not have chosen a more apt expression: "Fishers of men." It is an expression which awakens some very profound echoes among the boating people in the Sea of Galilee. If he had said, "I will make you preachers, or apostles, or priests," they would have understood nothing, and would have remained perplexed and irresolute. But to be fishers of men, that they can understand. Jesus knew how to tailor his catechesis to the situation. And thus Peter and Andrew left their nets behind and followed him. James and John, too, left their boat and their father Zebedee and followed him. They were setting out to fish upon the vast seas of the world. They did not know where it would all lead them, but with this man the fishing would be good. Jesus is the first great fisherman, the great catechist.

Jesus, show me where the fish are.

You know all the best spots:
    You know where the fish are to be found, along
    the shore or out in the deep,
    to the right or to the left.
Lord, take me to the fish.

36. Humor calms the storm

He said to the sea, "Be still" (Mk 4:35-41).

"The Master was in the stern, asleep on the cushion."
"Teacher, do you not care if we perish?" Christians, and
men of today, often speak as did the apostles during this
storm. In fact we often go even further than did the
disciples, with their fear and their lack of faith. We say,
"God is dead." I should like to think that "God is laughing" (cf. Ps 2:4).

During the day, Jesus, seated in Peter's boat, had
been preaching parables to a huge throng which was
crowding upon him at the shores of the lake. When
evening came, he decided to cross over to the other side
(December, A.D. 28). He set out just as he was, without
going ashore for any provisions or baggage. As skilled
fishermen, the apostles are in charge of the navigation.
Jesus takes advantage of this fact to catch a brief nap,
stretched out on the cushion in the stern of the small
boat. This is the only passage in the entire Gospel that
shows Jesus asleep. He had accomplished his work during the day, and now he could enjoy a legitimate rest.

But then a sudden storm arises. In winter the winds
have a way of whipping down rapidly upon the lake,
especially the northern part, in the neighborhood of
Capernaum. It is not uncommon at all to see, even within
the space of a half-hour, how the surface which had been
as calm and glassy as a sheet of oil, suddenly is covered

with mighty waves. This is followed by a sudden squall, and the waves begin to cover the little boat so that it is in danger of foundering. "Jesus was in the stern, asleep on the cushion." Accomplished sailors that they were, Peter, Andrew and company, they have lost all sense of direction and are mortally afraid. There is nothing more they can do but ask our Lord for help, with just a note of reproach: "Teacher, do you not care if we perish?" Just like Martha, when she complained of Mary's inactivity (no. 28).

Jesus wakes up. He rebukes the wind: "Quiet!" and the wind subsides. He speaks to the sea, "Be still," and a great calm ensues. These words of Jesus evoke the great words of creation, "God said . . . and so it was" (Gn 1:6).

Then, smiling, and with a touch of humor, he speaks to his disciples: "Why were you afraid? Have you no faith?" The disciples have faith indeed, but their faith was not strong enough, because they also had great fear, even though they were in the same boat as Jesus. Their faith was destined to be purified, to grow stronger. Later on, through the agency of the Holy Spirit, they would no longer fear anything, anybody, neither suffering nor death (cf. Ac 4:1-32). But today they have not yet "realized" that their Father in heaven is concerned for every hair on their head (Mt 10:30), and that even if Jesus is asleep, his heart is always watchful (Sg 5:2).

> Lord, are you asleep?
>   They say that you are dead.
> But I know that you are alive,
>   and that your Heart is watchful.
> Calm our storms.
> Lord, increase my faith.

37. Humor feeds the crowds

You give them something to eat (Mt 14:13-21).

Jesus is embarking for a desert place, away from people, on the other side of the lake, across from Capernaum (April, A.D. 29). Upon learning of this, the crowds leave their cities and villages behind and set out on foot, following the shoreline while the boat goes straight across the lake. Oblivious of distance and fatigue, without even thinking of provisions or lodging, they all set out to go hear Jesus. This fact speaks for itself. It shows the interest and attraction felt by the crowd for our Savior. Even though they often remained, on the surface, impulsive, and incapable of reflection, there is still no reason to suspect their true sentiments of faithfulness and genuine affection.

Upon disembarking, Jesus finds that the people have kept up with him. The crowd will not give him a moment's rest. Still Jesus experiences a feeling of tender compassion for them: he cures the sick, and speaks to the throngs. The hours pass, and Jesus does not seem to be aware of time. His disciples, finally, remind him that this is a desert place, that it is growing late, that these people must be hungry: "Send the crowds away to go into the villages and buy food for themselves."

Jesus answers, "They need not go away; you give them something to eat." Always the most simple words. Always this easy assurance on the part of Jesus, this calm and perfect self-mastery, where we cannot discern even the slightest agitation, the slightest hesitancy, the slightest show of nervousness. Always this same personable and condescending manner, slightly challenging and filled with humor, preparing the unwitting collaborators in the spectacle he is about to present.

Their answer: "We have only five loaves here and

two fish." This is very little, in fact it is nothing at all for a crowd of 5,000 men, not counting women and children. But this is the human collaboration which Jesus requires and needs in order to accomplish his divine work: the first multiplication of the loaves. Jesus gives the order for the crowds to sit down on the grass. He takes the five loaves and the two fish, raises his eyes to heaven, and speaks a blessing (like our benediction, like an offertory). Then, breaking the loaves, he gives them to the disciples, who take them, a little at a time, from the Lord's hands, these inexhaustible provisions, and distribute them to the crowds. There is enough for everyone, enough to fill them all. What is more, when they gather up the remnants of the loaves, there is enough to fill twelve baskets.

Of all the marvels performed by Jesus up to that day, this is perhaps the most surprising, because it is equivalent to an act of creation: "Let the earth produce . . . , let the waters teem with fish" (Gn 1). Still, neither Matthew nor the other evangelists seem to have been moved by such a show of power. There is not a cry of enthusiasm, not a word which departs from their ordinary calm and objectivity.

"You give them something to eat." The disciples had the pleasure of giving the food to the crowds. But they will never forget that it is from Jesus that this food has come. This is Jesus' way of preparing them to give, to every nation, his Body to eat and his Blood to drink (no. 39).

Lord, you ask me
    to give something to eat to those about me.
It is you who gives through me.
Multiply your love in me.
Multiply your humor in me.

38. Humor makes us walk

"Come," said **Jesus** (Mt 14:22-33).

After the multiplication of the loaves (no. 37), a frenzied reaction runs through the crowd: "Truly this man is the prophet who is to come into the world." They try to lay hold of him in order to make him king (cf. Jn 6:15f.). His disciples, won over by the enthusiasm of the populace, are no less favorable to this prospect. Jesus has to "constrain" them to re-embark and cross over to the other side, while he dismisses the crowds (Mt 14:22). Having thus sent them on their way, he climbed the mountainside in order to pray privately. The night had come and he remained there, all alone.

The boat had already reached the middle of the lake, where it was seriously buffeted by the waves, for the winds were contrary. From his solitary mountain, Jesus could easily imagine the effort required to maneuver that boat that night, when his followers had such a great need of rest. Still, he is in no hurry to help them: they must first have the experience of their own weakness and inability, and thus recover from their unthinking enthusiasm of the day before.

Finally the hour has come. At about the fourth watch of the night, towards dawn, Jesus sets off after them, walking upon the lake. Sailors are much more inclined to see ghosts than other people are, or so it is said. Credulous or not, the apostles are not deceived: there really is someone out there walking peacefully along, in their direction, upon the agitated waves. Seized with fear, they start to cry out. But Jesus tells them at once, "Take heart, it is I; have no fear." A ghost who speaks is not a ghost at all. What is more, it is obviously the voice of the Master. These are the familiar words which he will repeat so often.

Peter can no longer contain himself. A foolish idea has laid hold of his mind and heart. Like most people, of his kind, spontaneous and impulsive, without taking time to weigh the pros and cons, he launches into immediate activity: "Lord, if it is you, bid me come to you on the water." What a remarkable idea. But at the same time, what a powerful confidence in the omnipotence of the Master.

Jesus, smiling, takes him at his word: "Come." Under the startled eyes of his companions, Peter leaps from the boat and begins walking upon the water in the direction of Jesus. Everything goes well until the moment that he forgets about the Master and begins to think of the violence of the wind and the waves. He becomes afraid and begins to sink. At the very moment that he was about to reach the Master, poor Peter feels the yielding surface of the sea give way beneath him. He shouts out for help. Jesus immediately holds out his hand and grasps him: "Oh man of little faith, why did you doubt?" At Jesus' touch, the waves once again feel solid beneath his feet. Together they make their way back into the boat, and the wind dies down. Everyone in the boat worshipped him and said, "Truly you are the Son of God."

This event gives us a clear insight into Peter's real character, full of contrasts, so sympathetically human. This man who leaps upon the sea in the presence of his Master is the same man who is destined to confess him as "Christ, the son of the living God" (no. 40); the same man who, at Gethsemane, will not hesitate to draw his sword, all alone against a throng of armed enemies (no. 51). But this is also the man who, when he saw the wind, was afraid and began to sink; the man whom Jesus himself had to refer to as "satan" (no. 40);

the man who ran like a coward on the night of Jesus'
arrest (no. 51); and who denied his lord and his God
when questioned by the servant (no. 52). His story is
a sad and very human mixture of sublime daring and
incredible lapses.

Peter has a great amount of zeal, and "only a little"
faith. In his fervor, he is always ready to leap into
things: he walked on water, but only for a little bit,
a short distance, and then he began to sink. He needs
to experience his own weakness, in order to lean solely
and completely upon the strength of Jesus. The day
will come when he goes all the way to the very end.
Humor has made him walk.

> Lord, you tell me "Come."
>   I leap forward because you are calling me.
> But I hesitate because the wind is strong,
>   and I sink because I forget you.
> Still you keep your sense of humor:
>   you reach your hand to me with love,
> and you say: "Why did you doubt?"

39. Humor speaks the words of life

Will you also go away? (Jn 6:22-71).

The day after the multiplication of the loaves (no.
37), Jesus goes back to Capernaum, into the synagogue.
The crowds assemble there, curious and at the same
time satisfied at having "eaten bread to their fill." Still,
there are some "thinkers" among them, some who have
a "critical and incisive mind," and who insinuate the
notion that yesterday's miracle, while it was indeed
remarkable, was only a single isolated fact, and was
much less remarkable than what Moses had done, who
fed his people for forty years with manna in the desert.

When all is said and done, Moses is still to be preferred to this unknown man from Nazareth.

Jesus begins by setting everything in its proper sequence: it was not Moses who supplied the manna, the bread from heaven, but rather "my Father who gave it to you." What is more, when Jesus will give "his" manna, "his" bread, this will be not only for forty years, but this will be "a true bread which comes down from heaven," a bread which gives life to all the world, and for all times.

Those who have "the thoughts of men" (no. 40) can only think of a material manna which frees them of the obligation of working for their bread in the sweat of their brow. Their response is vulgar, on an earthly level: "Lord, give us this bread always." There is a kind of bittersweet irony in their tone, a little like that of Nicodemus (no. 33) or the Samaritan woman (no. 18).

But Jesus dominates the scene. He has something important to say, and he will say it. He goes on to reveal, progressively, and with insistence, something that is very familiar to us today, the mystery of the Eucharist. But for his audience this was an unheard of novelty. The opposition of the "intelligentsia" grows in pace with his revelation.

"I am the bread of life." The bread of heaven is not just bread made of flour and cooked in the oven: it is Someone, a Person, it is Me. In order to receive this bread you have only to come to me, to believe in me, "who have come down from heaven, sent by my Father."

These statements provoke a movement of protestation: "The Jews murmured at him, because he said, 'I am the bread which came down from heaven'." They murmured like the Jews in the desert (Ex 16:2). What Jesus has just told them about his heavenly origins is an enormous revelation. How can a man whose father and mother are well known attribute a heavenly origin to himself?

But Jesus disregards the objections which arise on every side. He does not explain, he merely states. Their reasoning will not lead them to any conclusions. They would do better to listen and to reflect. Jesus repeats, insistent: "I am the bread of life." For the second time, "this is the bread which comes down from heaven and whoever eats it does not die." The revelation progresses: They must "eat" Jesus. Up to this point, strictly speaking, it was possible to listen, to believe, to follow.

But here Jesus goes one step further, a step which only the Son of God could possibly take. Never has a Buddha, a Confucius, or a Mohammed ever dared to say "the bread which I shall give is my flesh for the life of the world." Many of the people understand, not without good reason, that all this must be taken in its literal sense as a sort of cannibalism, that what is involved is the physical act of eating his flesh—and they find the prospect absurd: "How can this man give us his flesh to eat?" Another of these famous questions "How?"—pretentious and insulting, addressed by man in the face of something God has done. Zachary says "How?" and is reduced to silence because he had spoken one word too many (Lk 1:18).

For the moment, Jesus does not take up the question of how this is to be done. What he wants is a true faith. He had told them previously that "this is the work of God, that you believe in him whom he has sent" (v. 29). His audience must believe in his person, in his word, and await from his good pleasure the eventual revelation of the "how."

Instead, he simply repeats his statement as to the necessity of eating his flesh. He deliberately accentuates the imperative, adding that they must drink "his blood," and he says this no fewer than four times. "Truly, truly, I say to you, unless you **eat the flesh** of the Son of Man and **drink his blood,** you have no life in you; he who **eats my flesh and drinks my blood** has eternal life, and I will raise him up on the last day. For my flesh is food indeed, and my blood is drink indeed. He who **eats my flesh and drinks my blood** abides in me, and I in him. As the living father sent me, and I live because of the Father, so he who **eats me** will live because of me. This is the bread which came down from heaven, not such as the fathers ate and died; he who eats this bread will live for ever" (vv. 53-58).

Jesus could not have insisted more, could not have been more clear or more explicit. The words which we translate from the Greek as "eat" could more accurately be rendered as "devour" or "crunch," with extreme realism. Jesus is doing his best to eliminate every possibility of figurative interpretation. The Father has entrusted the work of salvation to the Son, and Jesus means to realize this work with his own body and his own blood, which we are to eat and to drink, in order to have communion with him.

His audience understood him very well, and it was on this occasion that "the secret thoughts of their hearts" (Lk 2:35) are all revealed. The recalcitrant Jews are rooted even more in their disbelief: that was to be expected. As for the disciples who are more or less committed to the Master, many of them are simply shocked. Jesus' words seemed harsh and forbidding. They are thinking of eating flesh which has been reduced to the state of a corpse: a sort of necrophagia. And such a prospect is totally beyond them: "These words are too strong. Who can hear them?"

Jesus knows that many of his disciples have begun to murmur at these words: he does not need to be advised of this fact by anyone. Still, the true reason for their attitude is not to be sought in any theoretical difficulty: it rests simply with their lack of faith. The "reasons" are often only excuses for a lack of "heart." If they really had faith in Jesus, they would have accepted his words, even if the words appeared obscure. The Master denounces this scepticism which has spread even to his disciples. Still, he is not surprised at it: "Jesus knew from the beginning who they were who would not believe" (no. 17). For faith is a gift from the Father, not the conclusion of a reasoning process, nor any evidence based on human experience (no. 57). "After this many of his disciples drew back and no longer went about with him." This was the great defection, the crisis of the Galilean ministry, an anticipation of the crisis of the Passion itself.

The Twelve saw and understood everything: "To eat my flesh," "to drink my blood." But if they understood anything, they understood it on the same terms as those who were leaving. Despite their special selection, they too might choose to leave. Jesus invites them in a firm but affectionate tone of voice, to make a decision in the face of this proving: "Will you also go away?" They thus find themselves at one of those psychological moments which frequently decide the whole course of a human existence.

Simon Peter, as their true leader, is the first to answer, in the name of all the Twelve. His declaration is one of the most beautiful protestations of faithfulness that could possibly be conceived: "Lord, to whom shall we go? You have words of eternal life; and we have believed, and have come to know, that you are the Holy One of God." Peter and the apostles have no greater understanding than any of the others: our Lord's language is an enigma. They do not believe on the basis of the evidence for what he says, but rather on the basis of the authority and the truthfulness of him who speaks. They believe in the Master in whom they have recognized the Son of God, the Light of all the world. For them, the words of Jesus, repugnant as they might be to the human mind, are still words of life; they deserve and obtain their total commitment. This commitment, accordingly, is not based on the light of human reason, but on the light which proceeds from the Holy One of God, recognized as such by their human reason. And that is why their faith is true.

Jesus' statements about the Bread of Life have thus achieved their effect: faith. The work of God is accomplished in these few hearts which are nourished by the life-giving words which Jesus has spoken to them and which, through them, he will address to all the world.

It is only much later, a year later, that Jesus will reveal just how we are to eat his flesh and drink his blood. As a matter of fact, the promise of the Eucharist is located around April in the year 29. It will be on a Thursday evening, in April of the year 30, on the eve of his death (no. 46), when "Jesus loved his own even unto death," that he will tell them how: "Jesus, taking the bread, broke it, gave it to his disciples, and said, 'Take and eat; this is my body.' And taking the cup, he gave thanks and gave it to them, saying, 'Drink this all of you, for this is my blood, the blood of the new covenant . . . Do this in memory of me'" (Lk 22:19; Mk 14:22; Mt 26:26).

40. Without humor there can be no thought of God

Get behind me, Satan! (Mt 16:13-23).

"From that time (July, A.D. 29), Jesus began to show his disciples that he must go to Jerusalem and suffer many things from the elders and chief priests and scribes, and be killed, and on the third day be raised" (Mt 16:21).

Jesus had just asked his apostles, "But who do you say that I am?" And Peter had just answered, "You are the Christ, the Son of the Living God." And Christ had set up this apostle as the foundation of his Church: "You are Peter, and on this rock I will build my Church." It is at this moment, when Jesus has just elicited such a firm profession of faith from his apostles, that he makes the first prediction of his Passion. To the revelation of the glorious role of the Messiah, he now joins the proclamation of his suffering role, the accomplishment of the prophecy of Isaiah concerning the Suffering Servant. Through this form of pedagogy (no. 8), which will be reinforced a few days hence by his Transfiguration, followed in turn by a second proclamation of his Passion (Mt 17:22), Jesus is preparing the faith of his followers to face the approaching crisis of his condemnation and death.

Faced with such a prediction, Peter is scandalized, shocked, and, "taking hold of him," as if he meant to protect him and draw him away from danger, he cries out: "God forbid, Lord! This shall never happen to you." Peter is wrong, certainly not in his affection for the Master, but in his understanding of things divine.

"Jesus turned"; we might say that Jesus kept on walking while Peter was trying to hold him back, "taking hold of him and beginning to rebuke him." But then the Master turns to Peter with words of severe reproach: "Get behind me, Satan! You are a hindrance to me; for you are not on the side of God, but of men." Get behind me! Leave me alone! Go away! As if he were punishing a child, sending him to the rear of the class, putting him outside the group.

Satan! Peter must have been deeply struck by this choice of words. He could not have known that a year

and a half earlier someone had made a similar proposal
to Jesus. Someone who wanted to turn him aside from
the Messianic way of the cross with all its demands
for humility, suffering, and death—and that someone
was Satan. He too had warned Jesus: No! Not that way!
That is not proper for you! Choose rather the admiration of all mankind, which you can achieve by miraculous deeds and acrobatics. Seek rather the support of
the mighty and the kingdoms of this world with all
their splendor. And Jesus had given him precisely the
same response he gives to Peter: "Go away, Satan!"
(Mt 4:1-11).

"You are a hindrance (Greek: scandal)!" The word
"scandal" means a stone over which someone can trip
and fall. One commentator has remarked with judicious
subtlety: "At the very moment in which Jesus is going
to head towards Jerusalem to die there, Peter gets in
his way: he turns into an obstacle in the path, an obstacle which was in danger of tripping Jesus up. To
the rear with him! He had just been called the rock
of foundation, and now he is a stumbling block instead."

"You are not on the side of God, but of man." Peter
had just proclaimed his faith in Jesus as the Messiah,
the Son of God: this was truly on the side of God:
"Flesh and blood has not revealed this to you, but my
Father who is in heaven." But now, Peter balks at the
cross of the Master: this is the way men think, the
way that flesh and blood would think, in terms of
human reasoning, the way that Satan would think.
Peter had just been congratulated for the truthful ring
of his faith; but now he is reproached for the false note
emitted by his human mind. Peter is true gold, but not
yet purified. His purification will come, but only after
the terrible sequence of fault, repentance, and miraculous recovery, all through the strength of Christ, dead
and risen from the dead.

Lord, you see the whole course of my thinking:
> Thoughts that come from God, thoughts that
> come from man.
I would not dare to blame Peter:
> for I too am frightened at the cross.
Give me the gift of understanding your path
> which leads past the cross to the resurrection—
and to follow it
> with love and with humor.

41. Without humor, we speak at cross-purposes

Peter did not know what he was saying (Lk 9:28-36).

The evangelists locate the Transfiguration of Jesus about eight days after Peter's profession of faith, at Caesarea Philippi (no. 40). It is a confirmation, on the part of God himself, of the revelation made to the Apostles on the subject of Jesus' messianic mission and divinity. It also has as its purpose, by making Christ appear in glory, to strengthen the courage of his apostles, at a low ebb now through the prospect of Christ's Passion, and to show that the Lord Jesus already possesses the glory which his resurrection will only increase.

Jesus went up the mountain (probably Tabor) in order to pray, accompanied only by the three habitual companions, Peter, James and John (nos. 22, 50). The three of them fall asleep, just as they will do at Gethsemane. They are thus not witness to the beginnings of the transfiguration. But, suddenly starting out of their sleep, they are astounded to behold Jesus transfigured, conversing with two other persons, Moses and Elijah.

Peter is the first to speak (this is so characteristic of his temperament), interrupting Jesus, Moses, and

Elijah in their conversation. Nobody had asked him for his opinion, but it is characteristic of exuberant natures such as his to offer an opinion on every subject, frequently in a rather inconsiderate manner. Here, the naive suggestion of the apostle must make us smile: "Master, it is well that we are here; let us make three booths, one for you and one for Moses and one for Elijah." Overcome at the prospect of the Master's glory, he has lost the proper perspective on things.

"It is well that we are here." A first interpretation suggests itself in terms like this: we are better off here than on the difficult roads of upper Galilee, in the press and throng of the crowds, surrounded by the constant attacks and harassments of the Pharisees, better off than anywhere else, because Jesus is radiant with glory —and thus Peter would be thinking primarily of himself. But a second interpretation would lay stress rather on his hasty offer of cooperation: it is well that we are here in order to set up three booths of branches. Three will be enough. We can simply lie down where we are, in the open air. What he is suggesting is a sort of overnight camp, to shelter Jesus and his blessed guests. And thus Peter would be thinking primarily of other people. Nonetheless, "he did not know what he was saying."

"As he said this, a cloud came and overshadowed them; and they were afraid as they entered the cloud. And a voice came out of the cloud, saying, 'This is my Son, my Chosen; listen to him'." Just as he had on Sinai, God is now speaking through the midst of the cloud. He does not address himself to Jesus, but to the disciples, in order to present to them this Jesus as his well-beloved Son, his Chosen One. These words are an echo of Peter's profession of faith at Caesarea, a consecration of the revelation of the mystery of Christ as suffering and glorious. Claiming the divine sonship of Jesus,

God the Father adds these words: "Listen to him." Surely this is also addressed to Peter who, some few days earlier, had protested so violently against the prospect of the Passion.

Peter was never to forget what he had seen and heard on that mountain. In his second letter (1:16-18), he recalls the sources of his faith and his preaching of the Gospel: "We did not follow cleverly devised myths when we made known to you the power and coming of our Lord Jesus Christ, but we were eye witnesses of his majesty. For when he received honor and glory from God the Father and the voice was borne to him by the Majestic Glory, 'This is my beloved son, with whom I am well pleased,' we heard this voice borne from heaven, for we were with him on the holy mountain."

When Peter wrote this letter (around the year A.D. 64), he was head of the Christian community, "he knew what he was saying." He had even developed a sense of humor, because he wanted to be crucified upside down.

Lord, I am a little bit like Peter:
    often I do not know what I am saying.
    I build booths that will not last.
Give me the gift of listening to you.

42. Without humor there is quarreling

What are you discussing with them? (Mk 9:1-29).

It is the day after the Transfiguration. Rejoining the other disciples at the foot of the mountain, Jesus finds them in animated, almost violent conversation, with the scribes. A poor father has come looking for the apostles with his epileptic child. He had meant to ask the Master to heal him. But in the master's absence, at the insistence of the child's father, the apostles were trying to do it themselves. After all, had they not already been given authority over unclean spirits? (Mk 6:13). But they were able to achieve no results. We can well imagine the joy of the scribes, who always followed closely after Jesus in order to spy upon his deeds and his words and thus discredit and accuse him. For the apostles, this setback is all the more embarrassing because of the crowd. They were thus discussing the reasons for their failure, trying to determine the most effective method of forcing a mute demon to speak, the technique to be used in forcing him to reveal his name. Their discussion had turned into an argument.

It is at this point that Jesus, Peter, James and John make their arrival. The Master asks a question to which he already knows the answer, "What are you discussing with them?" The father explains his son's misfortune and the failure of the disciples. Jesus exclaims, "Oh faithless generation, how long am I to be with you? How long am I to bear with you?" These words, and other similar words, addressed primarily to the scribes, but also to the apostles (no. 2), reveal a new facet in Jesus, who is so "meek and humble of heart" in other circumstances (Mt 11:29).

Jesus' words, expressing such a poignant burst of sorrow, are aimed at everyone. The Word has come down from heaven. He has become incarnate in order to instruct us and to redeem us. And the closer he comes to the end of his career, the more he recognizes the emptiness of his efforts: his efforts with his apostles, who are so little inclined to prayer; his efforts with respect to the crowd, always eager for something extraordinary, always indifferent to true conversion; his efforts towards the scribes who are so eager to observe and criticize, but not to understand and amend their lives; his efforts in behalf of this father himself, for whom the failure of his disciples has considerably lessened the confidence he had in Jesus.

Nonetheless, in spite of his great weariness, a weariness not unlike that which a doctor might experience when people refuse to follow his prescriptions, Jesus. orders them to bring the child to him. The father, sensing that the cure of his child depends in the last analysis upon his own faith, now proclaims this faith. Fearing that this is not sufficient, he humbly begs Jesus to help his imperfect faith. The child is brought in. Jesus takes him by the hand and raises him up.

Once the crowds have left, the apostles find themselves alone with Jesus once again, in a nearby house. Their public failure weighs heavily on them, and they are eager to discover the reason behind it all. Jesus explains it to them, "This kind cannot be driven out by anything but prayer and fasting." There is a universal lesson to be gleaned from this incident, both for the apostles and for all those whoever have to work in behalf of the Kingdom. The apostles failed because they had too much confidence in themselves, and in the power which they received. They lost sight of the divine origins of this power. They had forgotten that they are only instruments, and that this power does not work like some magical technique, but rather that it demands a constant disposition of faith and humility and prayer. They and their successors are never to forget this fact, they are always to imitate Jesus, who himself constantly prayed, even though he had recourse to material means (Mk 7:31; 8:22). If the apostles have failed, they have only themselves to blame for their failure: they acted without having recourse to prayer which remains the one and only true "technique."

If there are still disputes among apostles, theologians, pastors, monks, nuns, Christians, non-Christians, all of us, might this not be because we pray too little?

Lord, it is you, you alone who save.
Do not let my failures, my mistakes, my sins
    ever diminish the faith of others.
Do not let our disputes
    impede the progress of your Kingdom.
Give us the gift of prayer, of dialogue,
    with your love and with your humor.

43. Humor unmasks idle ambition

What were you discussing on the way? (Mk 9:33-37).

Jesus and the Twelve have just arrived at Capernaum (September, A.D. 29). They make their way to a house which is described as "the" house (Peter's? Matthew's?). Entering, Jesus asks them, "What were you discussing on the way?" Jesus' tone betrays more knowledge than it expresses. The apostles, embarrassed, avoid a direct answer. Wasted effort on their part, however, since Jesus knows everything that was going on in their heart. On the way, they had been discussing among themselves who would be the greatest.

In order to grasp the full extent of the apostles' false ambition, we must recall that immediately before this incident, while they were walking towards the village, Jesus had spoken about the end of his life: "The Son of man will be delivered into the hands of men, and they will kill him; and when he is killed, after three days he will rise" (v. 31). But they did not understand the saying, and they were afraid to ask him. They could not understand how the Messiah, whom they had acclaimed in the person of Jesus, could possibly undergo

an ignominious death. What is more, they had completely lost sight of the glorious perspective of a resurrection after three days. Finally, they did not dare to ask
him any questions, perhaps for fear of prompting some
kind of reprimand, as had Peter (no. 40); perhaps, more
likely, because they were reluctant to learn the whole
truth and its demands upon them.

Frequently Jesus would walk all by himself, a short
distance ahead of the group (no. 40). The apostles quickly forget Jesus' teaching. Behind the Master's back,
the real concern of their hearts becomes the subject of
their discussion: "Who will be the greatest among us?"
Peter points out that he is the leader. John, that he is
the favorite. Judas stresses the fact that he carries the
purse. Each of them has some good reason to urge.

Jesus sits down and calls the Twelve to him. If he
asks them about the subject of their discussion, with
a touch of subtle humor, it is only in order to instruct
them, to make them progress, today we would say to
make them "develop." He does not insist upon the question under discussion. He passes on immediately to the
lesson. He does not even refer to the need for some
form of hierarchy. He himself had made Peter the head
of his Church (Mt 16:18). A little later he made the
Twelve the basis of the religious society which he had
founded (Mt 18:18). Today, he wants to show all of them
the spirit in which they must accept their promotion
and fulfill their obligations. With respect to all questions of dignity and preference, he has only one teaching: "If any one would be first, he must be last of all
and servant of all." He will return to the same concept
of authority as service, in discussing a further dispute
prompted by apostolic vanity (no. 45).

In St. Matthew (18:4) the lesson on the spirit of
childlike humility is very concise: "Whoever humbles
himself like this child, he is the greatest in the kingdom

of heaven." Still, neither his teaching on the first and the last, nor the living lesson of his own example seem to have been very long retained (no. 45). The lesson is, for all that, a valuable one, in Jesus' time, and even today.

> Lord, meek and humble of heart,
>   my conversations are often vain:
>   I think of myself, of how to make myself advance,
>   I think of others only in terms of my own
>   egotism.
> Jesus, help me to correct myself,
>   to become a child of the Father,
>   your brother, and the brother of all men.

44. Humor does not keep count

Seventy times seven! (Mt 18:21-22).

Jesus is a good mathematician (the number-one mathematician). He can count the number of hairs on my head (Mt 10:30). He can count the number of stars and call each one of them by its name (Ps 147:4). But when it comes to my sins, he forgives them and they do not count any more.

Where the difficulty enters in here, is when Jesus asks me to do the same thing with respect to my neighbor, when he invites me to say, "Forgive us our trespasses as we forgive those who trespass against us." I find Peter generous in proposing that he pardon as many as seven times. I have not yet encountered anyone who has offended me seven times, and I do not know what I would do in such a case.

But Jesus wants to go further, "Seventy times seven times." I must willingly admit that I have offended the Master more than 490 times. And each time, he has forgiven me. In his hymn of love, St. Paul says that love is not irritable or resentful (1 Cor 13:5).

> Our Father who art in heaven . . .
> Thy will be done.
> Forgive us our trespasses
> as we forgive those who trespass against us.

45. Humor invites us to serve

You do not know what you are asking (Mt 20:20-28).

Jesus is on the road to Jerusalem (end of March, A.D. 30). He is approaching the city of Jericho (no. 31). For the third time he announces to the Twelve how he will meet his end: "Behold, we are going up to Jerusalem; and the Son of Man will be delivered to the chief priests and scribes, and they will condemn him to death, and deliver him to the Gentiles to be mocked and scourged and crucified, and he will be raised on the third day" (Mt 20:17-19). It is "then" that the mother of the sons of Zebedee came out to him, together with her sons, and knelt down before him to make a request. "What do you want?" He asked her. "Command that these two sons of mine sit, one at your right and one at your left, in your kingdom." After the first proclamation of his Passion, Jesus had to listen to impetuous protestations from Peter (no. 40). After the second, the apostles began to discuss who would be the greatest among them (no. 43). After the third, James and John send their mother Salome to speak for them, just like Rebekah for Jacob (Gn 27:5), or Bathsheba for Solomon (1 K 1:15).

This episode makes it clear that, of all the disordered passions to which the Twelve were still subject, ambition remains the most tenacious, despite the constantly repeated warnings of the Master. Jesus' promise of the royal recompense that was reserved for their generous fidelity to his call had only whetted their desire for empty glory (Mt 19:28). The Twelve, he has told them, would be sitting at his side, on twelve thrones, to judge over the twelve tribes of Israel. But who would occupy the thrones closest to the King? This eagerness for the first position is pointed out in various passages in the Gospel (Mt 23:6; Lk 14:8).

If it is the mother who takes the initiative, her sons are certainly in harmony with her request. Perhaps it was they who put her up to the question. The Gospel text says that she came up to Jesus "together with her sons." She is proud of them: "These two sons of mine." All she is asking for them is simply that they should occupy the two most important positions, nothing more.

Jesus' answer is directed, not to the mother, but to the two ambitious apostles: "You do not know what you are asking." Our Lord must have smiled a sad sort of smile. What point was there in his constantly repeated admonitions; his disciples never seemed to understand anything. Left to their fishing, perhaps they never would have had any ambition beyond the shores of their little lake. But as apostles, here they were beginning to argue and quarrel about who would be first in the kingdom.

"Are you able to drink the cup that I am to drink?" This is the cup of suffering, ignominy, death. The sons of Zebedee suppose that the Master means to try their dispositions before promising them the positions that they covet. For these positions they are indeed prepared to make every sacrifice. Without any thought as to the contents of this cup, they answer with assurance: "We are able."

"When the Ten heard it, they were indignant at the two brothers." James and John, through the agency and complicity of their mother, were trying to insinuate themselves into Jesus' good graces, to assure themselves of the first positions, attempting thus to supplant their companions, even Andrew who was the first called, even Peter to whom Christ had promised the keys of the kingdom. This little troupe of men had already been infected with the ugly plague of discord caused by ambition. It was an infection which threatened to ruin them, to topple completely the hierarchy of the Church at its very formation. Jesus had a duty to save his Church, his hierarchy, his future work. He had to inculcate into his apostles some sense of humility in place of this vice of foolish vanity and ambition.

"You know that the rulers of the Gentiles lord it over them, and their great men exercise authority over them. It shall not be so among you; but whoever would be great among you must be your servant, and whoever would be first among you must be your slave." This lesson is addressed to the hierarchy of the Church and to all apostles of every age. The lesson springs up from the only source that could possibly produce it, the heart of Jesus himself, meek and humble, capable therefore of giving the one true advice for achieving humility and meekness. In the Kingdom of Christ, those who are called to lead others must consider themselves as the "servants" of their brethren.

Jesus goes on to say that "the Son of man came not to be served, but to serve." He, the Lord of heaven and earth, surely had the right "to demand that he be served" like all great kings and mighty persons. But he did nothing of the kind: he came in order to serve. Jesus has given the example; who can refuse?

Up to the very end, Jesus will continue to recall this lesson in humble service: "You call me Lord and Master, and you say well, for so I am. If then I have washed your feet, I the Lord and Master, then you too should wash

one another's feet. I have given you the example in order
that you may do as I have done to you" (no. 46).

> Lord, you have come in order to serve;
>   but I, I love to be served.
> I desire to be the first:
>   to do this, I must be the last.
> Help me to understand this.
> Help me to live,
>   with your love and with your humor.

V.

JESUS' HUMOR TO THE VERY END

Jesus loves his disciples "to the end" (Jn 13, 1). But, up to the very end, the apostles were slow to understand. And thus humor will have to be at work even during the tragic hours of the Passion, and continue even after the Resurrection, up until the Ascension (nos. 46-60).

46. Humor is understood, afterward (Jn 13:1-15).

Jesus, "having loved his own who were in the world, loved them to the end" (v. 1). In the course of the Last Supper, he got up from the table, laid aside his garments, excepting for a simple tunic, and girt himself with a towel, the insignia of a servant. He poured water into a basin, then he began to wash his apostles' feet and to wipe them with the towel around his waist. This was the office of a slave towards his master, even though the Israelite slaves were not constrained to perform it.

Jesus begins with Peter. If he had begun with someone else, Peter certainly would not have waited his turn to protest. The apostle's protestation is contained within the tone in which he speaks his words, "Lord, do you wash my feet?" It is more than a refusal, that would be meaningless: it is an impossibility. Every word is important: "Lord" stresses the dignity of Jesus. The two pronouns "you" and "my" underline the extreme contrast. "Wash my feet" indicates the humility of Jesus' service. Peter, as is his custom, follows his first impulse

with more impetuosity than reflection or humble sub-
mission to the Master's purpose. "What I am doing you
do not know now, but afterward you will understand."
That Peter does not understand, this is possible; he is
willing to accept the fact that he does not understand
everything. But still there has to be a limit. His repugnance at Christ's humiliation must have the last word:
"You shall never wash my feet."

"If I do not wash you, you have no part in me." Jesus
fully understands the character of his apostle. He starts
out by striking a responsive chord. It is the very impetuosity of his love that makes Peter resist him. Jesus now
appeals to this same love in order to achieve his sub-
mission. If Peter persists in his stubborn refusal, he
must break with the Master, and Jesus threatens to
withdraw his affection.

Once again we have the apostle's impetuous exag-
geration: "Lord, not my feet only, but also my hands
and my head." Even though Peter has not grasped Jesus'
entire thinking, he has grasped enough to abandon his
obstinacy. He goes from one extreme to the other. He
goes beyond the Master's invitation, offering his hands
and his head as well. The man who is unwilling to admit
that sometimes, in fact frequently, we must obey our
Lord simply and exactly without understanding everything involved, necessarily imposes his own "human"
initiative upon the divine plan, thereby thwarting it.

Afterward, when Jesus has put on his garments again
and everyone is sitting around the table once more, he
asks them, "Do you know what I have done to you? You
call me Teacher and Lord; and you are right, for so I
am. If I then, your Lord and Teacher, have washed your
feet, you also ought to wash one another's feet. For I
have given you an example, that you also should do as
I have done to you" (nos. 43, 45).

Lord, I would like to understand all at once,
    and yet you say "afterward."
    Help me to wait.
You ask me to follow you,
and you do not ask me to understand:
    excepting that you love me,
    and that I should serve you,
with your love and with your humor.

47. Humor in the face of ingratitude

What you are going to do, do quickly (Jn 13:21-32).

It is still Holy Thursday, during the course of the
Last Supper eaten by Jesus and the Twelve, one of whom
is about to become a traitor. After having explained his
reason for washing their feet (no. 46), Jesus seems to
have wanted to change the course of their conversation,
taking up the theme of their apostolate: "He who receives anyone whom I send receives me." But he did
not continue this theme. The sight of Judas, sitting or
reclining close to him, disturbs him. The plan which is
taking form in the mind of the traitor is a source of
horror to him. As in the Garden of Gethsemane, he is
suddenly overcome by his emotion: "Jesus was troubled
in spirit" and he said brusquely, "Truly, truly, I say to
you, one of you will betray me."

For a long time now, he had been saddened by Judas'
hardness of heart, by his ingratitude. Still, he had never
withdrawn from him all the initiatives of his love and
affection. Up to this point, Jesus had said nothing. But
now, as the event itself drew near, it was time to lift
the veil in order to prevent any scandal on the part of
his faithful followers. When the betrayal had actually
taken place, his disciples would remember that he had

told them of it in advance. This would be for them a further reason to believe in Jesus.

The disciples are astonished, and try to find out who it is. "Each of them knew his own conscience," says St. Augustine, "but since they could not read the secrets of any one else's heart, each of them was sure of himself but concerned about all the others, so that all of them were uncertain about each individual, while each individual was uncertain about all." The tension grew intolerable. Impetuous as usual, Peter can no longer contain himself; he wants an answer, cost what it may.

From his position behind Jesus, Peter makes a sign to John and suggests that he ask Jesus who it will be. The normal way of seating guests at dinner permits us to reconstruct the scene. (Peter at Jesus' right; John at Jesus' left; Judas at John's left). John, who only has to lean his head towards Jesus in order to whisper into his ear, turns his head and asks, "Lord, who is it?" Instead of pronouncing the traitor's name, Jesus answers with a sign, "It is he to whom I shall give this morsel when I have dipped it." Now this was a gesture of particular friendship, one which the giver of the dinner used to perform for certain special guests. So Jesus dipped the morsel and gave it to Judas, son of Simon the Iscariot.

"Then after the morsel, Satan entered into him." Satan was already there, to a certain degree, because it was Satan who had put it into Judas' heart to betray Jesus. But at this moment he takes complete possession; he carries Judas through to the fulfillment of his plan. The prince of evil finds no real resistance in the traitor's heart. The last scruples have been abandoned.

"What you are going to do, do quickly." This is not an invitation to evil, but rather the final word of an afflicted friend. None of the apostles, with the exception of Judas, —not even Peter and John—could possibly understand the real bearing of these words. Since Judas had control

of the purse for that small community (12:6), some of
the apostles supposed that he was being sent to buy provisions, or to distribute alms, since tomorrow was a festival day. The traitor took the morsel from Jesus, and
immediately went out.

"It was night." This is a detail which sets us thinking.
Outside, the night is dark and it swallows Judas up.
Inside, there is the radiant brightness of Jesus' final
words.

48. Humor in the face of impatience

You shall follow afterward (Jn 13:33-38).

These words, an echo of the "afterward" described
above (no. 46), are once again addressed to Peter. After
Judas' departure (no. 47), Jesus enjoys a few moments
of respite: "now is the Son of man glorified." The Passion
his already begun, insofar as Judas, under the impulse
of Satan, has just gone out. Jesus is already celebrating
his triumph as if it were accomplished (cf. 16:33).

For the last time, Jesus is speaking familiarly with
his apostles. "Little children," what gentleness in these
words! This introductory address sets the tone for the
entire "Last Supper discourse," which is really not so
much of a discourse as the outpourings of a heart filled
with love for his own. Filled with love, that is, for all
mankind. "Yet a little while I am with you. You will
seek me; and as I said to the Jews so now I say to you,
where I am going you cannot come." Where he is going
his followers cannot follow him at this time. He had
already told this to the Jews (7:34; 8:21). Now he repeats
it to his chosen disciples.

The hour of departure is always the time for final
instructions. Like a father on his deathbed, Jesus formu-
lates his last and most solemn will. He gives his disciples

a new commandment, which is to serve as their distinctive mark: "Love one another. Even as I have loved you, you also love one another." This commandment of Jesus is really "new" because it has for its model and its source the very love of Jesus for his own. He has loved us first. He always takes the first step, without being invited, without being put off by our ingratitude. He has not been sparing of any pain or suffering, or even of his life itself. He is number one in love (1 Jn 4:10).

"By this all men will know that you are my disciples, if you have love for one another." St. Thomas Aquinas makes this comment: "Whoever enlists in the army of a king must carry that king's insignia. Now the insignia of Christ is love. Whoever wants to belong to the army of Christ must, accordingly, be marked with the sign of love." They used to say of the first Christians, "see how they love each other, and how ready they are to give their life for each other." The world is so prepared to expect the radiance of this love of Jesus in his Church that it cannot possibly forgive the Church for any failure to demonstrate this love.

Peter has understood all this, but he is concerned only with the first part, "Where I am going you cannot come." From the point at which Jesus declared that where he was going his disciples could not follow him at that time, we might say that Peter was not listening to anything further. All of a sudden he explodes into the question that has been torturing him: "Lord, where are you going?" (another interruption on the part of Peter!) Jesus repeats what he had said previously, "Where I am going you cannot follow me now." But he adds a word of hope, "You shall follow afterward." Once again this mysterious and disturbing "afterward." For an impatient and impetuous man like Peter it means "too late." Why not right away? "I will lay down my life for you." I am afraid of nothing. Nothing can stop me, neither prison nor death. A fine protestation by a generous and loving spirit, but one which presumes too much on its own strength. "The spirit is willing, but the flesh is weak" (Mt 26:41). What Peter is lacking is a proper assessment of his own weakness which should make him seek his real strength, not in his zeal and impetuosity, nor in anything that is his, but rather in him who can make him strong (Ph 4:13).

"Will you lay down your life for me? Truly, truly, I say to you, the cock will not crow, till you have denied me three times." Poor Peter. He has not long to wait before the ultimate experience of his human weakness. In time, Peter will come to understand, and he will follow Jesus all the way to the cross, but this will be "afterward" (no. 60).

> Lord, always this "afterward" which is so irritating.
>   And yet you have waited for your "hour."
> Teach me to obey you simply,
>   exactly, at your good time.

49. Humor in the face of violence

It is enough (Lk 22:35-38).

We are at the end of this farewell dinner. Jesus gives one final word of advice to his apostles. He reminds them of his concern for them during the course of their three years together: "When I sent you out with no purse or bag or sandals, did you lack anything?" (Lk 10:4), and they answered all together, "Nothing." Up to this time, the apostles, under the protection of the Master, have been blessed. He had sent them on mission, advising them to carry nothing with them. The actual wording, "without purse, without bag, without sandals," was aimed at nothing more specific than a lesson in absolute detachment and trust in God. Even though they had brought nothing with them, neither did they need anything: everywhere they were well received.

We might be inclined to say that in the good old days something like this could very well happen. But these good old days do not last forever. Jesus is destined to leave. Everything will change. Hospitality will not always welcome the messengers of the Good Tidings: in fact, their audience will go so far as to put them in prison, to persecute them from one city to the next. They will have to be self-sufficient, surviving on their own resources: "But now, let him who has a purse take it, and likewise a bag."

What is more, they will find themselves surrounded by enemies, and they will have to defend themselves: "And let him who has no sword sell his mantle and buy one." The Master is not really recommending that his apostles resort to the use of violence; what he really wants is to warn them of a very critical situation in which violence will be commonplace. It is their allegiance to Jesus which will put the apostles into this dangerous situation. They will be despised and hated because of him. They are known everywhere as his most intimate disciples: they will be caught up in the same popular reaction that will crucify the Master. The apostles can count on no one but themselves in this dangerous crisis of their existence.

Interpreting Jesus' words literally, and in an attempt to show their courage and their determination to defend their Master, the apostles answer, "Look, Lord, here are two swords." Peter certainly has one of them: he will make use of it soon enough. But Jesus obviously has no intention of resorting to violence, nor encouraging his apostles to do so. He cuts the conversation short, "It is enough." The words seem to be an exclamation of powerlessness, perhaps impatience, in the face of their lack of understanding. This is frequently the sense of the word in English, and certainly the meaning of a word like **"Basta!"** in Italian. St. Cyril of Alexandria adds the comment that we are to interpret this response of Jesus as an indulgent smile, not without melancholy.

Peter has misunderstood, even Peter, or perhaps we should say, Peter first of all. He will enter into violent action a few hours later in the Garden of Gethsemane: "Then Simon Peter, having a sword, drew it and struck the high priest's slave and cut off his right ear" (Jn 18, 10). "Basta!"

> Lord, how often you have to say "enough"
>> to my ideas, to my plans,
>> where I have put more of myself than of you.
> Teach me to say "enough"
>> with Love and Humor.

50. Humor all by itself

Now you can sleep (Mt 26:36-46).

After the Last Supper, Jesus and his apostles crossed over the Valley of Kidron, and made their way to the foot of the Mount of Olives. They came to a place called Gethsemane, "the place of the oil press." Jesus leaves the group behind at the entry into the garden: "Sit here, while I go yonder and pray." He takes with him Peter, James, and John (nos. 22, 41). He begins to experience great sadness and agony. He tells them, "My soul is very sorrowful, even to death; remain here, and watch with me." All his life long, Jesus knew what was waiting for him at the end: "I have a baptism to be baptized with; and how I am constrained until it is accomplished!" (Lk 12:50). But on this night, the very imminence of the bloody sacrifice fills him with sorrow and agony.

Turning to his intimate followers, the Master asks for the comforting reassurance of their presence and their prayer: "Watch and pray."

Going on a little further, Jesus falls to the ground: the blessed humanity of Jesus collapses on the ground, his beautiful countenance soiled by the dust. He began to pray, "My Father, if it be possible, let this cup pass from me." He has taken on our human condition, with the exception of sin (Heb 4:15), without refusing the will of God the Father: "Nevertheless, not as I will, but as thou wilt." He returns to his disciples and finds them sound asleep, only a few feet from him as he experiences the most bitter struggles of his entire life. He speaks to Peter: "So, could you not watch with me one hour? Watch and pray that you may not enter into temptation; the spirit indeed is willing, but the flesh is weak." He speaks to Peter: all three deserve a reprimand, but Peter is the head, Peter is the one who has most need to pray, the one whose spirit is so willing, the one whose weakness is going to be evident within a very few hours.

Once again, for the second time, he goes on to pray: "My Father, if this cannot pass unless I drink it, thy will be done." Then he returns to find the three of them asleep once again. This time he says nothing: he leaves them sleeping.

A third time he prays. Perhaps it was this time that "being in an agony he prayed more earnestly; and his sweat became like great drops of blood falling down upon the ground" (Lk 22:44). He returns: his three friends are still asleep. He looks at them with sadness, but he does not wake them up; he says, as if speaking to himself: "Now you may sleep and take your rest. Behold, the hour is at hand, and the Son of Man is betrayed into the hands of sinners."

The words, "now you may sleep and take your rest"—

is this the humor of sadness, a tender irony, or indulgent kindness on the part of Christ? In the depth of the Master's heart, we can find all three at once: sadness at having been left alone by those whom he loved most; gentle irony, now that the time for them to watch has come and passed; you may sleep now if you want, the moment of trial has arrived and I must face it alone.

In his kindness, Jesus allows them to sleep a little longer, while he stays awake and prays. Then he awakens them: "Rise." As they take their time getting up from their heavy sleep, he adds: "Let us be going. See, my betrayer is at hand." As a matter of fact, while he was still speaking, Judas, one of the Twelve, came up, and with him a great crowd with swords and clubs.

> While you are in agony, how often do I sleep.
> While you are suffering, often I am doing nothing.
> Lord, teach me to watch and pray.

51. Humor in the face of betrayal

Judas, would you betray the Son of man with a kiss? (Lk 22:47-51).

Jesus was still speaking to Peter, James, and John (no. 50), when a great crowd arrived, magistrates and elders of the people, temple guards and Roman soldiers, fanatics and curious hangers-on. It is like a pack of ravening wolves all descending at once upon the divine Lamb.

At the head of this group walks Judas. The Gospel writers have refrained from describing the way he walks. They are content with pointing out that he was "one of the Twelve": this is enough to describe the radical perversity of his ingratitude. "Judas drew near to Jesus to kiss him." This was the customary mark of respect and affection between disciple and Master. This kiss, while it might hide his crime of treason from the eyes of everyone else, was the sign agreed upon to point out to the followers of the Jews who it was they were to arrest.

"Judas, would you betray the Son of man with a kiss?" Jesus knows that this kiss is the sign agreed upon to deliver him to his enemies. He accepts this first outrage, though it is more painful than all that is to follow: the kiss of a traitor whom he had always treated as a friend. These sad words are one final offering of grace as well as a rebuke: the name of Judas is pronounced with affection and sadness, the title of Son of man is a clear reference to the Messiah, and the Son of God—all this should have recalled this straying soul back to the intimacy which united him to the Master, all of this should have deeply touched his heart, if he had not been completely hardened in his sin. But once again, even Jesus' extreme kindness encounters blindness of heart.

Jesus then addresses the entire crowd, with an irony that is kingly and full of majesty: "Have you come out as against a robber, with swords and clubs? When I was with you day after day in the temple, you did not lay hands on me. But this is your hour, and the power of darkness" (vv. 52-53).

In this hour of turmoil and confusion, the luminous personality of Jesus dominates the entire scene, putting everything into its perspective: all that he is to suffer he will undergo willingly, peacefully, without ever for a single moment being dominated by the Prince of this world. "The prince of this world is coming. He has no power over me; but I do as the Father has commanded me, so that the world may know that I love the Father" (Jn 14:30-31).

52. Irony in the face of condemnation

If I have spoken wrongly ... If I have spoken rightly ...
(Jn 18:23).

All during the Passion, from Thursday night through Friday afternoon, in the presence of Caiaphas, Annas, Pilate, and Herod, the Lord Jesus speaks and acts like a king; he is the true master of his destiny. His dignity and his majesty, his words and his silence—they are an impressive spectacle for all. He stands above the hate of the chief priests, the lying testimony of the witnesses, the petty politics of Pilate, the frivolity of Herod, the cruelty of the torturers. He knows the secrets of everyone's heart. The thoughts and purposes of men believe that they can destroy him who is a source of embarrassment to them, but Jesus had predicted all this. It is he who freely guides the course of history: "I lay down my life of my own accord. No one takes it from me. I have power to lay it down, and I have power to take it again" (Jn 10:18).

The few words and the many silences of Jesus throughout this night of darkness are more eloquent than any commentary. The high priest questions Jesus about his disciples and his teaching. Our Lord responds, "Why do you ask me? Ask those who have heard me, what I said to them; they know what I have said" (Jn 18:21). The Master's irony judges his judges.

Jesus' answer leaves Caiaphas speechless. One of his zealous servants, in an effort to curry favor with his masters, strikes Jesus in the face and says, "Is that how you answer the high priest?" The Master retorts, "If I have spoken wrongly, bear witness to the wrong; but if I have spoken rightly, why do you strike me?" The dilemma involves an irony that cannot be answered.

The whole Sanhedrin are looking for a witness

against Jesus, in order to put him to death, but they cannot find one. Many people give false testimony against him, but their testimony is not consistent. Even Caiaphas tries his hand; he rises solemnly before the assembly and speaks formally to Jesus: "Do you make no answer?" "But Jesus kept still and would not answer anything" (Mk 14:61). The very silence of Jesus is an ironic condemnation of the lies of his detractors and the hypocrisy of his judges.

Pilate asks him: "Are you the king of the Jews?" "Do you say this of your own accord, or did others say it to you about me?" (Jn 18:34). Are you saying this yourself, or is somebody putting words into your mouth? Truly a majestic lesson to a Roman procurator who allows himself to be manipulated by an angry crowd.

This same Pilate now flaunts his authority: "Do you not know that I have power to release you, and power to crucify you?"—"You would have no power over me unless it had been given you from above" (Jn 19:11). You are but a tool in the hands of my Father.

At the sight of Jesus, Herod is filled with joy. For a long time he had hoped to see him. He expected to see him work a miracle. He questions him insistently; "But Jesus answered him nothing" (Lk 23:9). Faced with the frivolity of a Herod who was concerned only with the marvelous and the sensational, Jesus' irony takes on the form of silence.

In these hours of darkness, the irony of the Man-God suggests that of the Psalm (2:1-4): "Why do the nations conspire, and the people plot in vain? The kings of the earth set themselves, and the rulers take counsel together, against the Lord and his anointed . . . He who sits in the heavens laughs; the Lord has them in derision."

53. Humor in the face of prayer and pardon

Father, forgive them; for they know not what they do (Lk 23:34).

It is difficult to determine at precisely what moment Jesus spoke this prayer in behalf of those who had crucified him. It can even be assigned to some time during the act of crucifixion itself. Then it would take on a particular grandeur: "When they came to the place which was called the Skull, there they crucified him, and the criminals, one on the right and one on the left. And Jesus said, 'Father, forgive them; for they know not what they do'" (Lk 23:33-34).

It is an heroic prayer, a prayer spoken by the Man who is dying for those who are putting him to death. It is hard to imagine anything more magnanimous. There is such a contrast between the praying victim and the brutal executioners. In the original Greek, it says that Jesus "was saying," "was praying": the use of the imperfect tense would indicate a prayer that is either prolonged or repeated.

Jesus was praying: for the Roman soldiers who were nailing him to the cross, making fun of him, coming up to offer him a drink of vinegar, saying, "If you are the King of the Jews, save yourself" (Lk 23:36). The soldiers do not know what they are doing.

Jesus was praying: for those who were passing him by and making a mockery of him, wagging their heads and saying: "You who destroy the temple and build it in three days, save yourself! If you are the Son of God, come down from the cross" (Mt 27:39). "Father, forgive them, for they know not what they do."

Jesus was praying: for his two companions, one on the right, and the other on the left, while he hung in the middle as if he were the guiltiest of the three. One

of these criminals, hanging on the cross, also insulted
him, "Are you not the Christ? Save yourself and us"
(Lk 23:39). The criminal did not know what he was
doing.

Jesus was praying: for the high priests who, together
with the scribes and the elders of the people, were
mocking him and saying, "He saved others; he cannot
save himself. He is the King of Israel; let him come
down now from the cross, and we will believe in him.
He trusts in God; let God deliver him now, if he desires
him; for he said, 'I am the Son of God'" (Mt 27:41-43).
The high priests and the theologians do not know what
they are doing.

Jesus was praying for Pilate who, knowing him to be
innocent, had tried to set him free, but who, finally, in
his weakness and political ambition, had delivered him
up to be crucified. Jesus was praying: for Herod who,
together with his whole court, had treated him with
mockery and contempt (Lk 23:11). The politicians and
the "playboys" do not know what they are doing.

Jesus was praying: for all those who, over the course
of all centuries, would ever mock him and crucify him,
just as culpable, or perhaps even more culpable, than
those who were there on that Friday, on Calvary. We do
not know what we are doing.

Jesus experiences an unlimited love for all men, a
great sense of brotherly mercy. Do anything you want
to me, he seems to be telling us, provided that, in the
end, you understand who I am. All his life he preached
this doctrine: "Love your enemies, pray for those who
do evil to you" (Mt 5:44). And he put it into practice.
He also said, "Bless those who curse you, pray for those
who slander you" (Lk 6:28). Those who "hate him without reason" (Jn 15:25) have gathered to curse and slander
him and do their worst to hurt him. But he does not

blame them for it. He does not blame anyone. All he does is pray and bless.

54. Humor, the accomplice of a thief

Today you will be with me in Paradise (Lk 23:39-43).

Do we dare to speak of humor on Calvary? Is this not too solemn, too terrible a time for that? On such an occasion as this, is it not more proper to look defeated? (no. 14) to put away our smiles? (no. 4), in a word, to be really serious? And still, despite all this, St. Lawrence, on his gridiron, was able to say (obviously with humor) "I am done on this side; turn me over." And so I ask, what could be the source of this heroic humor, if not Humor itself, the humor of him who is "spiritual" in every situation, filled with spirit and with the Holy Spirit from beginning to end of his life on earth? If I am wrong in supposing that Jesus had a sense of humor even on the cross, then he will pardon me in keeping with his own prayer: "Forgive them; for they know not what they do."

Jesus was crucified between two brigands, thieves, criminals, perhaps even assassins. One of the criminals hanging on the cross was insulting him and mocking him: "Are you not the Christ? Save yourself, and us too." Embittered by his misfortune, more rebellious than resigned, he was attempting to distract himself from his torment and the prospect of his imminent death, by echoing the insults of the chief priests and soldiers (no. 53). The other criminal rebukes his colleague: "Do you not fear God, since you are under the same sentence of condemnation? And we indeed justly; for we are receiving the due reward of our deeds." What he is saying is this: Look, this is simply not the time for mockery. Our execution puts us into the hands of God, you ought to realize that. All three of us are facing the same punishment, but he—speaking of Jesus—"he has done nothing wrong." In recognizing his guilt, in bearing witness to the innocence of Jesus, he is suddenly transformed, converted, in fact, turned towards Jesus and towards God.

He is a Jew who has probably heard some vague report of Jesus' kingship, of his kingdom, if only through the mockery of the spectators and the title nailed onto the cross above that head crowned with thorns. There is a mystery here. He puts his trust in this Jesus who is suffering and praying with so much dignity and gentleness. "Blessed are you, for flesh and blood has not revealed this to you, but my Father who is in heaven" (cf. Mt 16:17). It is he who starts the exchange. He and Jesus are to speak together, brothers in the face of a common misfortune. Their words will take them beyond the brutal torment of their punishment and the savage mockery of the crowds: "Jesus, remember me when you come in your kingly power." An admirable request, dictated by faith and trust and humility, such as only a criminal could make. He calls Jesus by his name, "Everything that you demand in my name . . ." Do not forget me when you become a king. Think of me who am suffering together with you, who have been crucified together with you. He does not demand much, simply to be remembered.

And Jesus' answer: "Truly, I say to you, today you will be with me in paradise." The answer is simple, confident, assured. Before the sun sets, you will be with me, we will be together. You and me, together, that is paradise. It is only Jesus, the Man-God, crucified and dying, who could make such a statement. No one else could even think of the words.

The criminal is the first saint canonized while still

alive. And by Jesus himself! "The thieves and the harlots go into the kingdom of God before you" (Mt 21:31).
This criminal has been a thief, on earth, "up to the very
end," and now he has actually stolen heaven. And Jesus
has been his accomplice. This is the most sublime humor.

55. Humor and love in a single name

Mary! Rabboni! (Jn 20:11-18).

It is Easter Sunday morning, early (April 9, A.D. 30).
There is a good deal of movement, running back and
forth, between Jerusalem and the tomb where Jesus'
body has been laid on Friday evening. In all this coming
and going, Mary Magdalene has a role of the very first
importance. It is she who arrives first, with the other
women, even before sunrise (Lk 24:10). It is she who
realizes that the stone has been rolled away from the
tomb. It is she who runs back into the town to tell Peter
and John: "They have taken the Master from his tomb,
and we do not know where they have put him." The two
apostles hasten to the site. John, younger, faster, gets
there first. But out of deference he waits for Peter. The
linen cloths, the wrapping from around his head, all the
trappings of his burial are there, all neatly rolled up,
but Jesus himself is not there.

"He saw and he believed" (Jn 20:8). John confesses
that it was at this very moment, and not before, that he
first believed in Jesus' resurrection from the dead. He
believes before he sees Jesus alive, but not before he
has seen the empty tomb and the burial garments. It
would have been even more perfect to believe in the
resurrection on the word of Jesus himself, at the very
moment when he first predicted it, according to the
prophecies of the Scriptures (v. 9).
Neither what had been written nor what Jesus him-

self had said was enough to make the disciples have any
faith in the Resurrection. Jesus does not want to force
the human mind, to constrain his disciples to have faith,
like the faith that is forced upon demons or the souls
of the damned, or like the faith which he could have
wrested from the Jews if he had taken a position against
their Sanhedrin fortified with the glory of his resurrection. It is in this perspective that we must re-read the
parable of Lazarus and the rich man, especially the part
about the pointlessness of anyone's returning from the
dead to warn living people who are not ready to listen
(Lk 16:27-31). What Jesus wants is an intelligent and
free and unforced adherence; what he wants is a faith
that comes from heart and mind; a faith which does not
stop with man but goes all the way to God. He knows
how to wait and put up with the delays that are necessary for someone to make a free choice. That is why he
leaves his disciples in suspense, even his chosen few
among them, up to the end of this "third day" after his
death. St. John tells us, very confidentially, that he received his faith at the moment that he and Peter had
established the fact, in some sort of official way, that the
tomb was empty. Peter and John believe, and they return in silence.

Mary Magdalene stays there: "Mary stood weeping
outside the tomb." Hers is a troubled soul. Tears are
streaming down her face, and her sobbing can be heard
at a distance, like that of a woman who no longer knows
what she is doing or saying. Her thinking had not been
oriented towards the prospect of a resurrection: "They
have taken my Lord, and I do not know where they
have put him." They have taken "her" Lord! Mary is
no longer the quiet contemplative at Jesus' feet (no. 28).
Now she is only a sensitive and tormented heart, looking
here and there, stooping down for another look into the
empty tomb, straightening up to examine the garden

once again: she is disoriented because she has lost "her" Lord.

Half-way out of the tomb, Mary notices a silhouette. She does not recognize Jesus, just like the disciples on the road to Emmaus (no. 56). She sees without seeing, through her tears and the turmoil of her troubled thoughts. She has a fixed idea about someone having taken the body. "She turned around and saw Jesus standing, but she did not know that it was Jesus." Jesus repeats the angel's words: "Woman, why are you weeping? Whom do you seek?" Jesus invites her to trust in him, and offers his assistance.

Mary is still convinced that the man standing beside her, at such an early hour in the morning, could only be the custodian of the garden. Instead of answering him, she continues with her own line of thinking. Perhaps it is he who has carried away the body of the Lord, in order to get rid of it. In this case, let him tell her where he has put it and she will carry it back herself. "Sir, if you have carried him away, tell me where you have laid him, and I will take him away."

Receiving no answer to her request, Mary turns back towards the tomb, forgetting the stranger. At this very moment Jesus calls her by name, "Mariam!" This is the name of friendship, the name he used when he was a guest at her house, the name she loved to hear. Obviously Jesus spoke it in a way that would make her recognize, from the tone and intonation, that it was his voice.

Surprised to hear herself called by her name, and in this tone of voice, Mary comes to herself. It is he! "Rabboni!"—"My" Master. No elaborate statement here, but simply a cry that comes from the heart.

Mary, moved by all the instincts of her heart and all the inspirations of the Holy Spirit, responds to love with love. She throws herself down to take hold of Jesus' feet, and holds them in a tight embrace. There is a silence filled with joy and recognition. Jesus allows her to express her love and happiness. Brought back to the "reality" which is the Master, cured of all her turmoil and disturbance, re-established in her serenity, she now enters deeply into the mystery: she adores "in spirit and in truth" (no. 19): yes, in truth, Jesus in his glory is everything that he has ever said, he is indeed the Son of God!

It is within this perspective that we must understand Jesus' words: "Do not hold me, for I have not yet ascended to the Father; but go to my brethren and say to them, I am ascending to my Father and your Father, to my God and your God." In these simple words, Jesus invites Mary to be the bearer of the Good News to the apostles, his brethren. The message which he entrusts to her is not to announce his resurrection and his presence, but rather to proclaim that very soon Jesus will rise back up towards his Father and our Father (Ascension). "Mary Magdalene went and said to the disciples, 'I have seen the Lord,' and she told them that he had said these things to her."

According to the Gospels, Mary Magdalene, the sinful woman, is the first person to whom Jesus shows himself after his resurrection. But it is legitimate to suppose that Jesus' first manifestation was to his mother Mary, who had given him his life and who had followed him all the way to the cross. But we have no record of this apparition of Jesus to Mary: we cannot describe either the moment, nor the duration, nor any of the particulars. Why have the evangelists kept their silence here, especially St. John? Could it be that a mother's testimony, even if that mother were the Blessed Virgin Mary, might have appeared suspect among those who did not know her? On the other hand, John tells us that his Gospel does not tell everything.

The testimony of Mary Magdalene becomes one further illustration of the Lord's words: "Thieves (the Good Thief) and harlots (Mary Magdalene) go into the kingdom of heaven before you" (Mt 21:31).

Lord Jesus, living with us, in us,
    you call us by our name,
    with love, with humor.
Give us the gift of calling upon your name,
    every day of our life.

56. Humor wants to be invited

He appeared to be going further (Lk 24:13-35).

"That very day (the Sunday of the Resurrection) two disciples were going to a village named Emmaus, about seven miles from Jerusalem." Shaken and discouraged, they were talking together, discussing everything that had happened: Jesus' arrest, condemnation and death, the empty tomb, the report of the women who said they had seen two angels (vv. 11, 22).

Suddenly they were joined by a third traveler. He had also come from Jerusalem. He began to walk with them. They did not recognize him:[1] "Their eyes were kept from recognizing him." Jesus said, "What is this conversation which you are holding with each other

---

1—In the apparitions recounted by Luke and John, the disciples do not recognize the Lord at the outset, but only after he speaks to them, as in the case of Mary Magdalene (no. 55), or makes some gesture as he did for the disciples on the road to Emmaus. Since they did not yet have any faith in the Resurrection, they could not even dream that the Master was really there. The risen Christ, moreover, while he continues to remain one and the same person, now exists in a new state (no. 23b) which goes beyond the sense conditions of this world and gives him the power to change his outward form, as St. Mark tells us in speaking precisely of this apparition to the disciples of Emmaus: "After this he appeared in another form to two of them, as they were walking into the country" (Mk 16:12).

while you walk?" They come to a stop, "looking sad." Could this ignorance be feigned? Might this stranger perhaps be an enemy of Jesus? In their sorrow and astonishment, and with perhaps a touch of mistrust, they answer, "Are you the only visitor to Jerusalem who does not know the things that have happened there in these days?" The stranger pretends not to understand. He wants to lead them to reveal what they themselves think about these facts: "What things?"

The travelers are familiar with these things, up to a certain point: Jesus of Nazareth, a prophet mighty in deed and word before God and all the people, had been condemned to death, and crucified; then the tomb was discovered empty, and some women were the first to bring the news, but as for "himself," no one had yet seen him. Then, what they were really thinking: "We had hoped (notice the imperfect tense, their hopes had disappeared) that he was the one to redeem Israel. Yes, besides all this, it is now the third day since this happened." So we might as well go home. But, two days? They should have waited for the end of the third day before leaving: that would have been more logical. But how can one look for logic in a heart that is grieving, in a soul that is in turmoil?

Jesus reprimands them: "O foolish men, and slow of heart to believe all that the prophets have spoken." He might just as well have added, "And slow of heart to believe everything that I have said and predicted." They have no understanding because they have turned the Messiah into a partial, an incomplete, and hence false image. They have focused only on the glorious and nationalist side of the promise. They have forgotten, if they have ever thought of it, the suffering aspect, the international dimensions, the universal and cosmic aspects of the work of the Messiah: "Was it not necessary that the Christ should suffer these things and enter into his glory?"

The sufferings experienced by Jesus of Nazareth are not a proof that he is not the Christ: rather that they are the literal sign of his fulfilling the ancient prophecies. This is what he explains to them during the two hours of their walk together: the most perfect lesson in Bible interpretation ever given on this earth: "Beginning with Moses and all the prophets, he interprets to them in all the Scriptures the things concerning himself." (How instructive it would have been to take this all down on tape.) The stranger spoke at great length, putting all his heart into his discourse, and all the light of his intelligence. The more he speaks, the more the shadows disappear, the more their hope returns. It is so clear, so true, so comforting that they later ask each other, "Did not our hearts burn within us while he talked to us on the road, while he opened to us the Scriptures?"

As they arrived at the village, "Jesus pretended that he was going on further: he wanted to give Cleophas and his friend the opportunity and pleasure of offering hospitality to their traveling companion. In the case of Zachaeus, he had invited himself (no. 31). Today, he waits to be invited. The disciples do not disappoint him. They have enjoyed this man's company and his conversation too much to let him go. They insist, they urge him, "Stay with us, for it is towards evening and the day is now far spent."

Jesus enters their home to spend the evening with them. In honor of their guest, they invite him to preside at table. No sooner had they reclined, than Jesus took the bread, spoke the customary Jewish blessing over it, broke it, and gave it to them. At this very moment "their eyes were opened," as if wakening from a deep sleep.

"They recognized him": his instructions along the road had prepared them for it, and now the blessing and the breaking of the bread, so familiar to the Savior, was the final bit of understanding they need. Jesus immediately disappears from their earthly eyes. His visible presence is no longer necessary. A different kind of presence has been inaugurated.

> Remain with us, oh Lord:
>   for it is growing late,
>   and the day is already far spent.
> Rekindle our hearts along the road,
>   so that they discover you
>   in the Scriptures,
>   and in the breaking of the Bread.

57. Humor bares its heart

Put your hand in my side (Jn 20:19-29).

On Easter day, Jesus appeared to his Mother, to Mary Magdalene (no. 55), to the disciples on the road to Emmaus (no. 56), and to Peter (Lk 24:34). That same evening, he revealed himself to all the disciples gathered together: "The doors being shut where the disciples were, for fear of the Jews, Jesus came and stood among them and said to them, 'Peace be with you.' When he had said this, he showed them his hands and his side. Then the disciples were glad when they saw the Lord."

On that evening, Thomas, also called the Twin, was not with them when Jesus came. He had not been seen since the Friday before, Good Friday. During the course of the week, some of them encountered him in the streets of the city and told him, "We have seen the Lord." They recounted the entire apparition, without omitting a single detail. "The doors were closed, and all of a sudden he was there. He spoke to us the way he always does, Shalom! Peace be with you. He showed us his hands and his feet: we could see the marks of the nails. He even opened his tunic to let us see the wound left by the spear, alongside his heart."

The disciples are happy, talkative, enthusiastic. Thomas is skeptical: "Say what you will, I have no faith in your imaginings. If you have seen something, it is only a ghost. "But Thomas, what will make you believe?" "I will believe only if I touch, only if I touch. Unless I see in his hands the print of the nails, and place my finger in the mark of the nails, and place my hand in his side, I will not believe." That whole week long, despite the unanimous testimony of the others, even Peter, Thomas, sure of himself like any positivist who calls himself a realist, holds fast to his position.

Eight days after Easter, Peter calls the disciples together once again: they have to plan their return into Galilee, to the rendezvous set by the Master (Mt 28:10). This meeting, eight days after the great event, would be the first celebration of "the day of the Lord," with its commemoration of the Resurrection. Thomas is present, for he too is from Galilee.

The doors are all closed, just as on the preceding "Sunday." "Jesus came and stood among them and said, 'Peace be with you.' Then he said to Thomas, 'Put your finger here, and see my hands; and put out your hand, and place it in my side'." There were no other words of reproach, only the affectionate and yet urgent words: "Do not be faithless, but believing."

Did Thomas actually carry out his demands? Did he put his finger into Christ's hands, his hand into Christ's side? It would hardly seem so. In a single instant all his resistance and all his hesitation have disappeared. Under the influence of grace, visibly inspired, he makes a complete profession of faith: "My Lord and my God!" In the Man Jesus, he recognizes the invisible God. The last one of all the disciples to speak is the first to proclaim the lordship and divinity of the risen Jesus. Nor is it by accident that Thomas, doubting Thomas, should be the first to express himself in such clear terms.

Still there is one thing missing to Thomas' faith. Jesus points it out, "Have you believed because you have seen me? Blessed are those who have not seen and yet believe." Thomas' case raises a question: in what exactly does authentic faith consist? If Thomas believes "because" he sees, is this still a true faith? As a matter of fact, Thomas sees a sign, just as we see the Bread of the Eucharist, and he believes in an invisible reality. He sees the risen Jesus, and he believes in the Lord and God. Faith is a gift of God, not the conclusion of any human reasoning, nor the evidence of any sense experience. Jesus stressed this very well when, after Peter's profession of faith (Mt 16:17), he said: "Blessed are you, Simon Bar-Jona! For flesh and blood has not revealed this to you (that is, your own reasonings, your own experience), but my Father who is in heaven." Faith is a gift of the Father, a light which is far superior to all the evidence of our senses and our human reason.

It is true that the testimony of the other apostles should have been enough for Thomas: this is the testimony that most believers must be satisfied with. "Blessed are those who have not seen and yet believe." Those who, motivated by the witness of the apostles, will accept the light of revelation, without the support of sense experience, these are declared blessed. Not in the sense that they have achieved some little happiness, but rather because they are truly enlightened by God, capable of discerning the truth of Christ on the basis of evidence that is more spiritual and more powerful than any miracle. They have "more than reasons" to believe. We do not believe because we see. We believe because we accept the offer that God makes us to believe. The grace of this gift and this acceptance are to be had only by humble prayer.

> Lord Jesus, living with us, in us,
>   you open your Heart to us.
> Give us the power to draw from it
>   your love and your humor.

58. Humor goes back to the lake

Children, have you any fish? (Jn 21:1-14).

It is primarily in Galilee that Jesus manifests himself in a visible way. During the forty days between the Resurrection and the Ascension, the disciples must have passed at least thirty in this province where the Master told them to meet him (Mt 28:7). Christ's presence is not given any precise location: the confines of human existence no longer hold for him. He is wherever his followers are: "I am with you always" (Mt 28:20). He wants to be available to his followers, in some way, in order to demonstrate to them during these weeks, by a number of proofs, that he is truly alive. At the same time he wants to strengthen their faith and complete their instruction, "speaking of the kingdom of God" (Ac 1:3). It is on the shores of the Lake of Galilee that we find the first meeting between Jesus and his followers (no. 35); it is here too that we shall find the final meetings. "After this, Jesus revealed himself again to the disciples by the Sea of Tiberias."

"And he revealed himself in this way." Simon Peter, Thomas, Nathanael, James and John were together at Capernaum, probably in Peter's house. They were living together, praying together. They were thinking about the remarkable events of the last fifteen days. But they also had to eat. Peter, finding himself in his familiar surroundings, in his little house on the shore of the lake, decides to go fishing. And the others approve of the suggestion: "We shall go with you." They go out and get into Peter's boat (no. 35). They fish all that night, the best time for fishing, but with no results.

"Just as day was breaking, Jesus stood on the beach; yet the disciples did not know it was Jesus" (nos. 55, 56).

About 300 feet separates Jesus from the boat. He calls out to them, "Children, have you any fish?" This is the most natural question in the world to ask a fisherman. He might be a prospective customer for their wares. "Children" — this is the usual translation: we might translate it better as "fellows." a familiar and friendly word of address. The disciples' answer is a terse and simple "no."

At this moment, their nets were probably out to the left side of the boat. "Cast the net on the right side of the boat, and you will find some." Acting on this stranger's instructions, the fishermen decide to try their luck once more. Success comes immediately, and they take so many fish that they cannot pull in their net.

At this sign, with its clear reminiscence of another miraculous catch of fish at the very same lake (no. 35), John suddenly understands who this stranger is, Jesus. He says to Peter, "It is the Lord!" If it is John who is quickest to remember and deeper in his insights, it is Peter, in his turn, who has the greater sense of decision and readiness of execution. In order to get to the Lord's side even quicker, he casts himself into the water and makes his way as rapidly as he could towards the beach. Truly a brave heart, a faithful friend. The others, less impetuous, bring their boat to the shore, dragging behind them the net which they have still not managed to lift on board. Arrived at the water's edge, they leave everything and jump out of their boat.

"When they got out on land, they saw a charcoal fire there, with fish lying on it, and bread." They were overcome with surprise. What they saw was not a Lord full of majesty, but a simple companion preparing their breakfast, in exactly the same way they always did it for themselves. "Come and have breakfast." Everything is so very simple, just like good friends on a camping trip, with their campfire by the side of a good fishing lake. "You must be hungry," Jesus tells them, "Bring some of the fish that you have just caught." And what a catch, 153 fish.

It is Jesus who plays host. So much familiarity is beyond their comprehension. They can hardly believe that he has experienced a Good Friday or an Easter Sunday. Seeing their Master so simple, so accessible, the apostles want very much to ask him, "Is it really you?" But they know full well that it is he. "Jesus came and took the bread and gave it to them, and so also the fish." It is always the same Jesus, always attentive to his disciples' needs. The resurrection has not changed the underlying attitude of his heart. But what an exquisite way to express it.

Lord Jesus, living with us, in us,
    simple and accessible,
you are the same yesterday, today, and forever.
Give us the gift of serving as you do,
    very simply,
    with your love and with your humor.

59. Humor calls for love

Simon, do you love me? (Jn 21:15-17).

Jesus says to Simon Peter, "Simon, son of John, do you love me more than these?" It is easy to recognize that Peter's triple profession of love corresponds to his triple denial of the Master. But we should be careful not to refer to this as a reinstatement of Peter. From Jesus' point of view, nothing has changed, Peter is loved as he has always been loved. But Peter, himself, no doubt needed to be reconfirmed in his own eyes and in the eyes of his brethren. This is what endows this simple conversation with such a sense of grandeur and tender friendship.

The first question might well have been made during their little meal (no. 58), when Peter, overcome at Jesus' gift of bread and fish, looks at the Lord with his eyes filled with affection and respect. By asking whether he loves him "more than these" (John, James, Thomas, Nathanael), Jesus seems to be pursuing a two-fold objective. First of all, he wants to show that Peter's pre-eminence of authority has to go hand in hand with the first Pope's greater degree of love. Then too, he wants to give Peter an opportunity to redeem his three-fold failing in the face of his brethren. Peter responds with touching humility. For the rest of his life, he will trust himself much less. He does not dare to claim that his is a greater love than that of his brethren. He leaves it up to the Master "who knows what is in the heart of man" (no. 6): "Lord, you know that I love you."

Jesus tells him, "Feed my lambs." The second and third time, the words are different: "Feed my sheep." There is no reason to suppose that the lambs refer to the simple faithful while the sheep refer to the other apostles. But the change in expression certainly shows that the Good Shepherd's flock, in its totality (Jn 10: 1-16), is entrusted to Peter's hands. What is at question, accordingly, is the delegation of a true primacy of pastoral authority over the universal Church. Just as he promised Peter that he would make him the unshakable rock foundation of his Church (no. 40), so now he consecrates him the shepherd of the whole flock of the elect. After having invested him with perpetuity, he now entrusts him with the universality of his Church. The abiding solidity of the rock was tied up with the firmness of his faith, his understanding of Jesus' true identity. The universality of his role as shepherd is bound up with the high quality of his love, the profound reality of his attachment to the person of Jesus.

There is nothing to indicate that these three questions followed in rapid succession, that there was not rather an interval between them, to make a stronger impression. The whole conversation unrolls in a solemn manner, as Jesus intended, but it is not forced. Even in his Resurrection, Jesus retains that simple, sometimes teasing, and always hearty nobility, not without a touch of humor.

Peter is disturbed by the fact that Jesus asks him a third time, "Do you love me?" His emotion suddenly gets the better of him. After everything that has happened, the Master has good enough reason to put him to the test. But still, he knows everything, and he knows how great a love now fills the heart of Peter. The poor disciple cannot help himself. He asks for mercy. He is hurt at Jesus' insistence, just as he was hurt when Jesus looked at him after his denial. But today he is less disturbed: in fact, he actually appeals to that searching look of Christ itself, and takes it as his secure place of refuge: "Lord, you know everything, you know that I love you."

Lord, you know all my many denials,
    more numerous than those of Peter.
Still, you come to me every day,
    to beg for my love.
You know everything:
    you know that I try to love you.

60. Humor is for all ages

When you were young . . .
When you are old . . . (Jn 21:18).

"When you are young." It seems that Peter was at about the middle of his life, between two ages, perhaps around forty. "When you were young, you girded yourself and walked where you would." To gird oneself, to prepare to walk wherever one wills—this is the mark of independence.

"But when you are old." The Savior appears to be promising him a long career, many years of life. "When you are old, you will stretch out your hands, and another will gird you and carry you where you do not wish to go." This is the gesture of the old man who raises his arms to allow someone else to put on his belt, and to lead him wherever they are going.

But Jesus' words are mysterious. They were not understood until after Peter's death. Peter's stretching forth his hands represented his crucifixion. Letting himself be girt by some one else and carried where he did not wish to go—this referred to his being tied to a cross with bonds, and led to the place of execution, or raised up upon the gibbet.

Peter was thus informed by Jesus himself "by what death he was to glorify God." Puzzling though these words must have seemed to the other disciples, the words of Christ cannot have completely escaped Peter. He understands, at the very least, that Jesus is commanding him to follow, to the point of sacrifice, as he had already predicted: "You will follow me afterwards" (no. 48). Moreover, this is something that Peter himself wanted and looked forward to: "I shall give my life for you" (Jn 13:37).

When St. John wrote his Gospel, around the year 100,

he knew exactly how his dear friend had died sometime
between A.D. 64 and 67. He himself adds a parenthesis:
"This he said to show by what death he was to glorify
God."

> Lord Jesus, living with us, in us,
> when I was young, I was serious.
> Now that I have become old,
> > I write about your humor.
> It might be that, like Peter,
> > I die upside down.
> Give me the grace to die
> > exactly as you wish,
> > and in your arms,
> with your love,
> > and with humor.

VI.

JESUS' HUMOR TODAY, IN US, THROUGH US

As long as there are people on earth, as long as we confuse the essential and the accidental, the absolute and the relative, here below we shall have need of Jesus' humor. Yesterday, today, and always, Jesus treats us with love and with humor. But today he is knocking at the door of our heart, asking us to love each other as he loved us. Today, it is in us and through us that he wants to exercise his gift of humor (no. 61).

61. Humor today, in us, through us

Today this scripture has been fulfilled in your hearing (Lk 4:21).

The need for humor. We need humor always, everywhere: at Jesus' time, and today as well (for today too is a time of Jesus). Everywhere people take themselves too seriously. Things were going badly "in those days" (Ep 5:16), just as things can go badly today. There was a wicked generation in those days (Mt 12:45), just as there is one today. The difference is that today we have become more aware, perhaps because we are more aware of things in general (!), more inclined to understand psychology (?), more intelligent (?). Is the world more wicked? There is no real reason to believe so. But the mass media are with us every day, every hour, every moment, forcing us to share the agony of every country, every nation near or far. They force us to experience the misery of the poorest quarters, the violence and struggle of all kinds of wars and battles. In our time, as in the time of Christ, it is good to hear the gospel of humor.

What is humor? Humor cannot be defined. It is too subtle, too deep-seated a reality to be captured in any verbal formula. If love is the bond of all perfection, the source of all spiritual brightness, then humor is the joy, the charm, the gentleness, the attraction, the salt, the light, the taste.

Christian humor. Christian humor, in the following of Christ, is based on a realistic optimism, a hearty good sense, considerable knowledge of self, of others, of God. The true Christian, a branch on the vine of Jesus, alive with Jesus' own dynamism, looks upon shortcomings, his own and those of other people as well, with an indulgent sort of irony, and smiles at them. The Christian who desires true spiritual development (that is, the Christian who is in search of perfection) starts out by seeing himself and others exactly as he is, exactly as they are: preoccupied with self, vain, ambitious, covetous, domineering, trying to fool God himself—something that cannot be done. The man who has a gift for humor uncovers certain sore places in modern society, both in some "tottering" old men and some "eager" young men, with a vigor that might well prove to be a little cutting, but is always motivated by love. Such a person is steeped with a sense of zeal that both burns and illuminates, like Jesus when he drove the money changers from the temple. What he wants to do is make people abandon their pettiness in order to find their true joy in God. The man who has a sense of humor is full of love: it is a tender love, and not affected. It is a gentle love but it has a dorsal fin, it is a humble love but it is full of dignity.

To laugh at oneself. The Christian with a sense of humor does not take himself too seriously. He laughs in spite of everything. Above all else, he knows how to laugh at himself. He knows that he himself has all the failings he finds in other people. And he knows that he does not see them all in himself. That is why he is so inclined towards mercy. That is why he takes Jesus seriously when Jesus speaks of the straw in someone else's eye and the two-by-four in our own eye (Mt 7:4). To laugh at other people is often a sign of mockery. To laugh with other people can be a sign of humor. But to laugh at oneself, this is certainly a gift of humor.

False humor. Christian humor, which has its source in Jesus, is not that "black humor" which calls attention to the absurdity of man and the absurdity of this world in terms of cruelty, bitterness, and sometimes even despair. Christian humor is never an irresponsible cynicism, no more than it could ever be vain and spiteful mockery. To have a sense of humor does not mean exactly "to think of something witty to say." The man who has a sense of humor starts out laughing at himself; the man who has the gift of wit laughs at other people, but is unwilling for them to laugh at him. Wit can be cynical; humor is always "meek and humble of heart." The devil can have wit, but never humor.

Fundamental humor. Christian humor is the Spirit sent by Jesus, the Spirit who spreads his love in human hearts and his understanding in human minds. It is the Spirit who spreads his fruits: joy, peace, patience, kindness, goodness, faithfulness, gentleness, self-control (Gal 5:22). Jesus has given us a new commandment: "Love one another, just as I have loved you" (Jn 13:34). The word "just as" means that we should imitate him, follow his example. This also means love and humor "together with" him who helps me as a friend. This also means love and humor "in" him, for Jesus wants to be the source of our love and of our humor. Jesus wants to love "through" our hearts. He wants us to supply whatever is lacking of his love and of his humor in their manifestations to the people of our world today. The Christian should be able to live and say with St. Paul: "It is no longer I who live, and love, but Christ who lives and loves in me. The life I now live in the flesh I live by the faith, the love, and the humor of the Son of God" (cf. Gal 2:20). And again: "In my love and in my humor I complete what is lacking in the love and humor of Jesus" (cf. Col 1:24).

For our time. Really, it would be good if the gospel of love and humor could be proclaimed in the face of the struggles and wars between our modern egotistical states. It would be a good thing if Communists and capitalists both could learn how to laugh and smile, together, at the genuine failings, at everything that is taken too seriously in their systems. It would be an excellent idea for management and union leaders, both of them, not to take themselves so seriously, and to take the real interests of the working classes much more seriously. It would be marvelous if politicians, journalists, professors, intellectuals, and "experts" of every category had a little less wit and a little more humor. It would be a very evangelical event if all Christians, Pope, bishops, priests, monks, nuns, and the simple faithful (as if all these others were not faithful!) would live the love and humor of Jesus. It would be nice to proclaim a day of humor, or even a week, or better still a whole year, an entire lifetime. If each and every one of us were convinced that he is not the only intelligent person, the only one with a sense of justice, the only one who possesses the Holy Spirit and the use of common sense,—if each and every one of us were to laugh and smile more at himself and less at other people, this would be the Kingdom of Jesus already come and established.

The service of humor. There is a sort of mystery and service of humor. It consists more in living than in preaching, so that everyone can learn to live, to suffer, even to die in a true spirit of faith and hope and love.

Leprosy does not offer any attraction for a person. When Father Damien discovered that he was a leper, he was satisfied with one simple observation: "Very well, instead of beginning my sermons with the words 'Dear Lepers,' I can now say, 'We lepers'."

Nobody enjoys the prospect of watching his most cherished plans fall apart. When St. Philip Neri encountered a serious obstacle, he used to say, "Thank you, Lord, from all my heart, because my plans are not going as I will, but rather as you will." We, on the other hand, are much more likely to demand that the will of the Father be done in heaven as it is on earth, and not on earth as it is in heaven.

St. Thomas More, as he was about to ascend the gallows, had this to say to the master of the Tower, "Help me climb up. I can manage the trip down by myself."

The Blessed John Kemble, on the day of his execution, asked for a brief respite in order to finish his prayers first, and then to enjoy one more good pipe. It is not required that a man smoke a pipe in order to become a saint, but such self-control in the face of death, and in the face of intense suffering, is a perfect example of holiness and full personal spiritual development. Only humor is truly brave, because it knows how to deal with the one absolute.

One of the victims that fell into the hands of the Chinese Communists was the young Chiao. He was a pleasant young man. Brought before the assembly where he was formally accused, and forced to kneel, he answered, "I kneel only before my God." He was severely beaten and forced to his knees. After the hearing, they commanded him to stand up. "I am sorry," he told them, "but I have not finished praying to my God."

The night before he announced the Council, Pope John XXIII recalls that he was hardly able to get to sleep. "John, why are you not asleep? Is it you, the Pope, or is it the Holy Spirit who governs the Church? It is the Holy Spirit, is it not? Very well then, sleep, John!"

Humor has a way of making a person gentle, and keeping him in a joyous state, even if fortune goes against him. "A saint who is sad is a sad saint," said St. Francis de Sales. Instead of "saint," we might as well say "Christian, man, woman."

The pessimist says:
   my glass is half empty.
The optimist says:
   my glass is half full.

The pessimist says:
   God is dead.
The optimist says:
   Christ is alive.

EPILOGUE˙

Jesus performed many other acts and said many other words that evidence his love and humor, which are not related in this book.

If we were to describe in detail the whole of Jesus' love and humor, yesterday, today, and for all eternity, I suppose that the world itself could not contain the books that would be written. What is written in this book has been written so that you would believe that Jesus is the Christ, the Son of God, the first and the last in humor, the alpha and the omega in love, and that believing you may have life in his name, in the dynamic force of Love and Humor.